Broke to Wealth

How To Build a Strong Financial Foundation, Implement Effective Strategies, and Sustain Financial Growth

By

Tanya Taylor, CPA, MBA

Award Winning Author

Copyright © 2024 Tanya Taylor.

All rights reserved, including the right to reproduce this book or portions thereof in any form whatsoever.

No part of this publication may be reproduced, stored in a retrieval system, or transmitted in any form or by any means, electronic, mechanical, photocopying, recording, scanning or otherwise, except as permitted under Section 107 or 108 of the 1976 United States Copyright Act.

Limit of Liability/Disclaimer of Warranty: While the author has used her best efforts in preparing this book, no representations or warranties are made with respect to the accuracy or completeness of the contents of this book and specifically disclaim any implied warranties of merchantability or fitness for a particular purpose. The advice and strategies contained herein may not be suitable for your situation. You should consult with a professional where appropriate. The author shall not be liable for any loss of profit or any other commercial damages, including but not limited to special, incidental, consequential, or other damages. If legal advice or other expert assistance is required, the services of a competent professional person should be sought.

Contents

Foreword --- vii

Acknowledgments --- ix

Introduction: Build Wealth and Live Your Best Life ---------------------- x

Part One: Building a Strong Financial Foundation ----------------------- 1

Chapter One: Setting Clear Goals --------------------------------------- 2

    What exactly is an Action Plan? ------------------------------------- 3
    Why Do You Need an Action Plan? ------------------------------------- 3
    What Makes Up an Action Plan? --------------------------------------- 4
    Crafting Your Action Plan --- 5
    Establishing Risk Strategies and Setting Long-Term Goals ------------ 8
    Setting Long-Term Goals -- 11
    Aligning Strategies with Long-Term Goals --------------------------- 13
    Exploring Insurance Vehicles and Aligning Goals with Financial Protection ---- 13
    Reflection --- 17

Chapter Two: Understanding and Managing Debt -------------------------- 20

    Types of Debt -- 20
    Tracking and Identifying All Debts --------------------------------- 23
    Prioritizing Repayment and Utilizing Debt Payoff Strategies -------- 26
    Consolidation and Negotiation with Creditors ----------------------- 29
    Improving Credit and Building a Strong Credit Score ---------------- 34
    Reflection --- 36

Chapter Three: Establishing Financial Security ------------------------ 38

    Retirement Plans and Maximizing Contributions ---------------------- 38
    Defining Investment Goals and Understanding Investment Principles -- 52

Learning to Invest and Research Investment Options ---------------------------- 53
Embracing Diversity in Investments --- 54
Creating a Diversified Portfolio: -- 55

Chapter Four: Cultivating A Mindset for Success ---------------------------- 58

The Psychology of Money and How Our Mindset Affects Financial Decisions - 59
Common Mindset Blocks To Financial Success And How To Overcome Them 60
Strategies For Cultivating A Mindset Of Abundance And Financial
Empowerment -- 62
The Role Of Visualization And Affirmations In Goal
Setting And Achieving Financial Success --- 63
Organizing Financial Documents and Establishing a Filing System -------------- 66
Tips for organizing financial documents,
including using digital tools and systems -- 67
Reflecting on Achievements and Adjusting Goals as Necessary ----------------- 70
Reflection -- 73

Part Two: Implementing Effective Financial Strategies -------------------- 76

Chapter Five: Mastering Budgeting and Spending Habits ----------------- 77

Tracking All Your Spending and Identifying Areas for Improvement ------------ 78
Creating a Budget or Spending Plan Based on Income and Expenses ---------- 83
Managing Spending Effectively and Adjusting Your Budget as Needed --------- 86
Strategies for Saving and Investing Surplus Funds ------------------------------- 88
Reflections -- 90

Chapter Six: Building an Emergency Fund ---------------------------------- 93

Difference Between Emergency Funds and Other Savings Accounts ----------- 94
Building Your Emergency Fund: Starting Strong with What You Have ---------- 96
Tips to Manage Expenses Without Tapping Your Emergency Fund:
Facing the Unexpected --- 97
Revisiting and Adjusting: Why Your Emergency Fund Needs to Evolve ------- 100
Common Challenges in Building an Emergency
Fund and How to Address Them --- 103
Reflection -- 103

Contents

Chapter Seven: Increased Income and Entrepreneurship — 106

The Relationship Between Income and Financial Stability — 108
How to Assess Your Current Income and Identify Areas for Improvement — 109
Expanding Your Income Horizons: Side Hustles, Investments, and Passive Income — 111
Strategies for Negotiating Salary or Freelance Rates — 117
From Idea to Opportunity: Generating, Evaluating, and Capitalizing on Business Ideas — 120
Reflection — 123

Chapter Eight: Investing For the Future — 126

ABCs of Investment: Risk, Return, Diversification, and Asset Allocation — 126
Aligning Your Investments with Your Goals: Prioritizing for the Future — 131
Why Aligning Risk, Time Horizon, and Investment Goals is Crucial — 133
Investment Options: Building Your Financial Toolbox — 135
Investment Strategies — 137
Choosing the Right Mix — 138
Keeping Your Portfolio on Track: Monitoring, Adjusting, and Staying Up-to-date — 142
Reflection — 145

Part Three: Sustaining Financial Growth and Stability — 148

Chapter Nine: Securing Financial Independence — 149

Why Financial Independence Matters: Owning Your Future — 149
Assessing Your Current Financial Situation — 150
A Comprehensive Roadmap For Financial Independence — 152
Steps to Achieve Financial Independence — 154
Reflection — 162

Chapter Ten: Navigating Economic Challenges — 164

Understanding Economic Cycles and their Impact on Personal Finances — 166
Recognizing the Economic Cycle and Adjusting Your Finances — 167
Tactics for Managing Financial Challenges During Economic Downturns — 170
How to Identify Opportunities for Financial Growth

During Economic Expansion -------- 172
Staying Disciplined and Avoiding Financial Pitfalls
During Times of Economic Growth -------- 174
Reflection -------- 176

Chapter Eleven: Cultivating Financial Wellness -------- 178

The Relationship Between Physical and Mental Health
and Financial Wellness -------- 179
Incorporating Health into Financial Planning -------- 181
How to Manage Stress and Anxiety Related to Finances -------- 182
How Reducing Stress Can Improve Financial Decision
Making and Overall Well-Being -------- 186
Investing in Personal Growth and Development
for Long-Term Financial Wellness -------- 188
Reflection -------- 190

Chapter Twelve: Giving Back and Leaving a Legacy -------- 192

The Ripple Effect: Giving Back and Finding Fulfillment -------- 193
Making a Difference: Ways to Give Back and Find Your Cause -------- 196
Establishing a Legacy Plan for Future Generations -------- 198
The Importance of Aligning Your Financial Goals with
Your Values and Priorities -------- 202
Reflection -------- 204
Key Takeaways -------- 205

Moving Forward Together: The Ripple Effect of Financial Literacy -------- 207

Beyond the Numbers -------- 208
Financial Literacy is a Journey -------- 208
Taking Action: Turning Knowledge into Progress -------- 209
Final Thoughts and Inspiration -------- 210
Confidence and a Positive Mindset -------- 210
A Call to Action -------- 210

Foreword

Broke to Wealth, by Tanya Taylor lays out an easy-to-follow roadmap that helps you to finally understand how to set financial goals and, more importantly, how to remain consistent and achieve them. No jargon or overwhelming numbers. Just a genuine desire to empower you to take control of your finances, while striking a balance between wealth building, finding your passion, and giving back – because wealth is not just about money.

Who better than Tanya to provide these practical and implementable strategies? She started her journey with an impoverished childhood in Jamaica, moving to New York City alone at 16, undocumented and with only $100. From there, she built an amazing professional career in the banking and insurance industries, while pursuing her passion for teaching others about personal finance for over two decades. True to her beliefs, she has built an admirable net worth while traveling to over 60 countries.

This priceless financial guidance is designed for you whether you are drowning in debt, barely scraping by, or simply seeking to optimize your financial health. What is your dream? Broke to Wealth will help you define that dream and, more importantly, show you exactly how to make it a reality.

Success isn't about relying on magic formulas, but about establishing a solid foundation. With the three-part structure that Tanya has laid out, you will easily see yourself moving from stuck and unsure to building wealth with confidence.

Here's what the essence of the book takes you through, step-by-step:

1. How to build a strong financial foundation.

2. How to implement effective financial strategies.

3. How to sustain financial growth.

While no single book will change your life, the action steps created in this book will shift your thinking and provide you with the tools to make transformative changes.

I highly recommend Tanya and Broke to Wealth!

Raymond Aaron

New York Times Best Selling Author

Acknowledgements

I would like to extend a very special thank you to Eva and Rupert Francis, my parents, who gave me wings to fly, even when they were filled with fear. To my amazing daughters, Alana, and Jordyn, who inspire and challenge me daily to show up and be my best self. I am also deeply grateful to my family, clients, friends, and members of the Grow Your Wealth Community, whose stories have helped to shape the contents of this book.

Introduction

Build Wealth and Live Your Best Life

> *"Having the right tools would give you the confidence to take action and change your financial future."*
> — **Tanya Taylor**

Do you feel like your finances are in a perpetual game of whack-a-mole? Every month, unexpected bills land like sucker punches, while grocery prices seem to climb faster than a toddler on a sugar rush. Is the dream of financial independence fading faster than your bank account balance?

Sounds familiar? You're not alone. Countless people struggle with money matters, feeling trapped in a cycle of debt and stress. But what if I told you there's another way?

Last year, I spoke to a broad cross-section of women and men, ranging in age from 24 to 65, concerning the state of their finances—whether their company offered education or they received any knowledge from school or family (for the younger age group). The overwhelming answer to these questions was that they lacked sufficient financial education. Surprisingly, even high-earning executives, making multiples of six figures, were facing financial challenges without a clear path forward.

The discussions were sometimes heartbreaking. I had one woman tell me she was worth more being dead than becoming disabled. She was an executive at a tech firm making multiple six figures. She had young children.

It was truly alarming to hear story after story, echoing the same distressing theme. I discovered a few straightforward actions that these individuals could immediately implement to initiate positive changes in their financial situations.

Imagine...

- Waking up without that knot of worry in your stomach.
- Traveling to exotic destinations without breaking the bank.
- Finally, achieving that financial goal you've been dreaming of.

This isn't some get-rich-quick scheme with fancy jargon and impossible promises. This is your **personalized roadmap to financial empowerment**. Forget dry lectures and spreadsheets – think of this as your **treasure map**, guiding you on an **exciting adventure**.

Whether you're a student juggling ramen noodles or a seasoned professional feeling overwhelmed. This book has something for you. **Let me show you how to:**

- **Ignite your financial adventure and design a future that excites you:** Ditch the generic "save more" advice and set goals that inspire you – visualize that trip to Peru or a down payment on your first home.

- **Create a spending plan that empowers you, not restricts you**: No more ramen noodles! Create a spending plan that works for you, not against you, and finally feel in control of your finances.

- **Sharpen your financial sword and conquer your debts like a champion**: Learn battle-tested strategies to conquer your student loans and other debts, freeing up cash for your dreams.

- **Turn small change into big bucks with investing strategies for even beginners**: Discover the magic of compound interest and watch your wealth grow, even on a student budget.

This book isn't just about numbers and calculations (although those have their place too!). It's about **changing your mindset, taking control, and feeling confident about your future.** I'll share stories of people who used these very strategies to transform their lives, proving that you can, too!

Now, you might wonder, "Why should I listen to what this book says about personal finance?" That's a fair question. After all, there are plenty of so-called experts out there offering financial advice.

Well, let me tell you a little bit about myself. For 24 years, I've worn many hats in the financial world: crunching numbers as an auditor, navigating markets with traders, mastering technical accounting, and even guarding the system as a regulator. I started an investment club, started a tax practice with my husband, have been teaching people how to manage their money, and have been practicing the strategies mentioned in this book.

It is how I managed to save over *one million dollars* for retirement before I was 48 years old and got featured in major publications like 'Business Insider' and 'Black Enterprise'. I also saved for my children's college—very important.

While building a comfortable retirement portfolio (crossing that 7-figure mark!), I haven't sacrificed adventure. 60 countries and 29 states later, I can confidently say I've balanced financial goals with exploring the world and spending quality time with family.

But my life didn't start there. I was 16 years old when I came to America alone. I was undocumented. I had $100. I lived with family friends whom I met for the first time. For 7 years, I did not have my own bed. As a matter of fact, I never had my own bed until the age of 25, when I purchased my first home. I went through extreme hardships financially where if I didn't eat at home before I left, I would remain hungry until I got back home from school and work. Although I worked in establishments where they sold food, I would still go hungry many days because I needed every penny. Only the sheer will to lift myself and my family out of poverty kept me driven.

I've experienced the highs and lows, the successes and setbacks. And through it all, I've learned a thing or two about what works and what doesn't when managing money. In this book, I want to share those exact strategies with you.

But don't just take my word for it. Along the way, I've had the privilege of helping others navigate their financial challenges. I've seen people go from drowning in debt to achieving their financial goals. I've witnessed firsthand the transformative power of taking control of your finances.

So, when I share advice in this book, it's not just fluff. It's based on real-life and proven strategies that helped me and others win. Think of me as your guide, cheerleader, and money buddy on your path to financial freedom.

Together, we'll conquer your financial worries and build a brighter, more secure future. Whether you plan to retire early, volunteer your time, or do whatever it is that you would love to do. For me, it's traveling the world. Don't wait another day! Let's embark on this journey with trust and the rock-solid belief that we can all achieve our goals if we are committed.

Part One

Building a Strong Financial Foundation

"Building a strong financial foundation is like constructing a sturdy lighthouse. It weathers the storms of unexpected expenses, illuminates the path to your dreams, and guides you toward a secure future. Each brick you lay, be it a thoughtful budget, a disciplined savings plan, or the relentless pursuit of debt repayment, strengthens the structure. And as you stand on the balcony of financial stability, you can finally appreciate the vast and vibrant sea of opportunity that stretches before you"

Chapter One

Setting Clear Goals

"Setting goals is the first step in turning the invisible into the visible."
—Tony Robbins

Imagine standing at the edge of a vast, uncharted forest. You know that somewhere within lies a hidden treasure waiting to be discovered. But to find it, you need a map—a clear action plan. This forest represents your financial journey, and the treasure is your ultimate financial goal.

Like exploring a forest, achieving financial success requires careful planning and setting short-term goals. But then, "Financial Success" is a phrase that shimmers with possibilities—beach vacations and early retirements. And for many of us, that dream remains out of reach, shrouded in a mist of unspoken fear. We all experience the reluctance to take the first step, the quiet resistance to setting goals that could unlock our financial freedom.

Fear, of course, rarely comes in its true colors. It masquerades as practicality, brings doubts about our abilities, and paints the unknown future of uncertainty. We tell ourselves, "Maybe next year," or, "It's too risky," clinging to familiarity, even if it's far from fulfilling. But are these justifications or simply excuses?

Ask yourself, are you truly better off today than you were a year ago? Are your finances moving closer to your dream life, or are you simply treading water? Ignoring the truth won't change it. If you're not actively progressing, the future you desire won't magically appear.

Setting financial goals isn't about blind leaps into the unknown; it's about creating a map, a deliberate plan that empowers you to reach your destination. These goals act as milestones on your journey, guiding you through the twists and turns of life's financial terrain. So, let's spotlight those fears, dissect them, and discover how to chart a course toward the financial freedom we all crave.

What exactly is an Action Plan?

An action plan is a written document that outlines specific steps you need to take to achieve a goal. It breaks down your goal into smaller, manageable tasks -- short-term goals -- and assigns responsibilities and deadlines for each task. You can turn your dreams into actionable steps that move you closer to your goals by creating an action plan.

Why Do You Need an Action Plan?

- **Clarity and Focus:** An action plan helps you clarify your goals and focus on what needs to be done to achieve them. It prevents you from feeling overwhelmed by breaking down your goals into manageable tasks.

- **Motivation and Accountability:** When you have an action plan, you know exactly what you must do daily to move closer to your goals. This can motivate you to take action and hold yourself accountable for your progress.

- **Efficiency and Productivity:** An action plan helps you prioritize your tasks and allocate your time and resources effectively. It ensures that you are working on the most important tasks that will have the biggest impact on your goals.

- **Measurable Progress:** By setting specific deadlines and milestones in your action plan, you can track your progress and see how far you've come. This can boost your confidence and keep you motivated to continue working towards your goals.

What Makes Up an Action Plan?

An effective action plan consists of several key components:

1. **Specific Goals:** Your goals should be clear, precise, and well-defined. Instead of saying, "I want to save money," specify how much you want to save and by when.

2. **Actionable Steps:** Break down your goals into actionable tasks. Each step should be concrete, measurable, and achievable. For example, if your goal is to save $1,000 in six months, your actionable steps might include setting aside a specific amount of money from each paycheck or cutting back on non-essential expenses.

3. **Timeline:** Establish a timeline for completing each task. Setting deadlines creates a sense of urgency and helps you stay on track. Be realistic about the time it will take to accomplish each step.

4. **Resources Needed:** Identify the resources, whether financial, informational, or human, that you'll need to achieve your goals.

This could include budgeting tools, educational materials, or support from friends and family.

5. **Measurement and Evaluation:** Define how you'll measure progress towards your goals. Track your achievements regularly and adjust your action plan as needed based on your results.

Crafting Your Action Plan

Now that you understand the importance of an action plan, let's dive into how you can create one for your short-term financial goals, before we do the same for long-term goals. A great way to ensure your action plan is effective is to use the SMART principle. This means that your goals must be **S**pecific, **M**easurable, **A**chievable, **R**elevant, and **T**ime-bound.

Now, here are the steps to follow to craft your action plan while utilizing the SMART principle:

Step 1: Define Your Specific Goals

Begin by stating what you want to achieve. Just as discussed above in our action plan, rather than saying, "I want to save money," specify the amount and purpose. For example, "I want to save $1,000 towards the down payment on a car within six months".

Step 2: Make Your Goals Measurable

Your goals should be quantifiable so that you can track your progress. Set specific targets for how to measure your progress. For instance, if your goal is to pay off debt, specify the exact amount you aim to eliminate. For example, "I want to pay off $5,000 in credit card debt within one year by paying $416.67 every month."

Step 3: Ensure Your Goals Are Achievable

Set goals that are within your reach and capabilities. Consider your resources, skills, and limitations. If your goal is to increase your income, assess whether it's feasible given your current job or if you need to explore alternative income streams.

Step 4: Make Your Goals Relevant

Ensure that your goals align with your overall objectives and values. They should be meaningful and relevant to your life. For one, if your long-term goal is to retire comfortably, your short-term goal of saving for a vacation may not be directly relevant unless it contributes to your overall financial well-being. Alternatively, if you have a goal to purchase a home within a year to generate rental income, this would be in line with your long-term goal because not only can you invest the rental income and let it grow as one of your retirement funds, but you can also live off that income in retirement while enjoying property appreciation.

Step 5: Set Time-Bound Deadlines

Establish deadlines for achieving each goal to create a sense of urgency and accountability. Break down your goals into smaller milestones with specific deadlines. If your goal is to build an emergency fund, set a deadline for saving a certain amount each month until you reach your target.

Step 6: Break Down Your Goals into Actionable Steps

Identify the specific actions you need to take to reach each goal. Break them down into smaller, manageable tasks. For instance, if your goal is to start a side business, your actionable steps may include researching business ideas, creating a business plan, and setting up a marketing strategy.

Step 7: Assign Responsibilities (if applicable)

If your goals involve multiple people or require collaboration, clarify who is responsible for each task. Assigning responsibilities ensures accountability and prevents misunderstandings. Let's say you're saving for a family vacation. Specifying who will oversee researching travel deals, budgeting expenses, and booking accommodations is the ideal thing to do.

Step 8: Monitor and Review Your Progress Regularly

Regularly review your action plan to track your progress and make any necessary adjustments. Celebrate small and large milestones and stay flexible in adapting to changing circumstances. To give an example, if you realize that you're not saving enough each month to reach your goal, reassess your budget and find areas where you can cut expenses or increase income.

Establishing Risk Strategies and Setting Long-Term Goals

With your action plan in hand and your short-term goals mapped out, it's time to zoom out and focus on the grander scheme. While setting long-term goals is pivotal for your financial roadmap, it's just as vital to identify the hurdles that might loom ahead – recognizing these risks early and creating strategies to overcome them will enhance your ability to achieve your long-term aspirations.

Identifying Potential Risks

Setting goals, both long and short-term, requires more than just envisioning your desired outcome; it involves understanding the challenges and uncertainties that may arise. **Here are some common risks to consider:**

- **Unexpected Expenses:** Emergencies such as car repairs, medical bills, or home maintenance can derail your financial plans if you're unprepared.

- **Job Loss:** A sudden loss of income can significantly impact your ability to meet your financial obligations and may require you to tweak your goals.

- **Health Issues:** Medical emergencies or long-term health issues can lead to unforeseen expenses and affect your ability to earn income. It is one of the biggest factors responsible for personal bankruptcy filings in the U.S.

- **Market Fluctuations:** Economic or investment market changes can impact the value of your assets and investments.

Analyzing Each Risk

Once you've identified potential risks, it's important to assess the likelihood of each risk occurring and the impact it could have on your goals. **Consider the following questions:**

- How likely is it that this risk will occur?
- What would be the financial impact if this risk were to happen?
- How would this risk affect your ability to achieve your short-term goals and progress towards your long-term goals?

Prioritizing Risks

Not all risks are equal, and it's essential to prioritize them based on their likelihood and potential impact. Focus on addressing the most probable and impactful risks first. By prioritizing risks, you can allocate your resources and efforts wisely to mitigate them.

Brainstorming Ways to Minimize Risks

For each risk you've identified, brainstorm potential actions you can take to minimize its impact or likelihood of occurrence. Consider both preventive measures and reactive strategies that you can implement to address the risk. For example, if the risk of job loss is a concern, you could focus on building an emergency fund to cover living expenses during unemployment, or you may invest in acquiring transferable skills that increase your employability in the job market.

Examples of Risk-Mitigation Strategies

- **Building an Emergency Fund:** Setting aside savings to cover unexpected expenses or income disruptions.

- **Diversifying Investments:** Spreading investments across different asset classes to reduce the impact of market fluctuations.

- **Having Multiple Income Streams:** Generating income from various sources to lessen dependence on a single source of revenue.

- **Learning transferable skills:** Acquiring skills that are in demand across different industries to enhance job security and career flexibility (Creating a Contingency Plan).

In addition to preventive measures, it's essential to have a contingency plan in place for each identified risk. A contingency plan outlines the specific actions you'll take if a particular risk materializes. This plan provides you with a roadmap for responding to unforeseen events and helps minimize the negative consequences for your financial well-being.

Components of a Contingency Plan

- **Identify Triggers:** Define specific events or circumstances that would indicate the risk has materialized.

- **Determine Actions:** Outline the steps you'll take in response to the risk, including financial, logistical, and emotional considerations.

- **Establish Timelines:** Set deadlines for implementing each action to ensure a timely response to the risk.

- **Review and Update:** Regularly review and update your contingency plan to reflect changes in your circumstances or new risks that may arise.

Setting Long-Term Goals

One of my clients sought my advice on her financial future. She was eager to invest in the stock market but felt overwhelmed by the idea. After a thoughtful conversation, I helped her see the importance of setting long-term financial goals. We discussed her aspirations, including owning a business and achieving financial independence.

By breaking down these lofty ambitions into smaller, actionable steps and incorporating short-term goals like saving a specific amount each month, she felt more empowered and focused. This approach not only clarified her path to investing but also gave her a sense of control over her financial journey.

Long-term goals help you stay focused on the bigger picture and ensure that your short-term actions align with your overarching objectives. **Here's how to set meaningful long-term goals:**

1. **Think Beyond Immediate Needs and Wants:** When setting long-term goals, it's essential to look beyond your immediate desires and consider your future self and aspirations. Reflect on what truly matters to you and what you envision for your life in the years and months to come. Whether it's achieving financial independence, retiring early, starting your own business, or supporting loved ones, your long-term goals should reflect your deepest aspirations and values.

2. **Consider Your Future Self and Aspirations:** Imagine yourself five, ten, or even twenty years down the line. What do you hope to have accomplished by then? What kind of lifestyle do you

aspire to lead? By envisioning your future self, you can gain clarity on your long-term goals and the steps needed to achieve them. Whether it's traveling the world, pursuing a passion project, or leaving a legacy for future generations, let your aspirations guide your goal-setting process.

3. **Break down Long-Term Goals into Manageable Milestones (short-term goals):** Long-term goals can feel daunting if viewed as distant objectives. Break them down into smaller milestones or targets to make them more manageable and achievable. By dividing your long-term goals into bite-sized pieces, you can stay motivated and focused on making incremental progress. Celebrate each milestone you reach, knowing that you're one step closer to realizing your long-term vision.

Achieving these long-term goals can bring a sense of fulfillment and accomplishment. Imagine the joy of stepping into your dream home, starting a successful business, or enjoying a comfortable retirement. Setting and achieving long-term goals not only improves your financial future but also enriches your life in meaningful ways.

For my client, we set a short-term goal to build an emergency fund and pay off debt. She reduced spending on designer clothes that sat in her closet unworn and stopped eating out as frequently. While paying down the debt, she began building her emergency fund. Once the debt was paid off, we created an investment account, and she began investing in the stock market.

Finally, we worked on her resume and interviewing skills. She interviewed for and got the job she didn't think she was qualified for. The 40% salary increase went towards further bolstering the emergency fund, investing, and paying for vacations with cash instead of credit cards. All this happened in under eight months.

Aligning Strategies with Long-Term Goals

As you develop task and risk strategies and set long-term goals, it's crucial to ensure that your strategies align with your overarching vision for the future. **Here's how align and adjust as needed:**

1. **Ensure Your Strategies Support Your Long-Term Vision:** Make sure that the actions you take today are in line with your long-term goals. For example, building an emergency fund can help reduce financial stress and provide a safety net, allowing you to take bigger risks later for larger goals such as starting a business or investing in real estate.

2. **Review and Adjust Your Strategies:** Regularly review your strategies to ensure they are still relevant and effective in helping you achieve your long-term goals. As your goals evolve and circumstances change, be prepared to adjust your strategies accordingly. Flexibility and adaptability are key to staying on track toward your financial objectives.

Exploring Insurance Vehicles and Aligning Goals with Financial Protection

By now, you have drawn out an effective action plan, set your goals, assessed the risks that might be involved in your situation, and found ways to mitigate those risks; these are all great, but there is one last thing you must do: the icing on the cake.

I'll come out plain with this: you can put things in place to try to avoid or reduce the impact of any risky event, but those strategies would only go so far. You can ease yourself from the pressure of having to rigorously plan for risk by setting in place a system that offers protection—it's like cruising on autopilot instead of having to fly with great effort. That protection is insurance.

Let me say this. I don't think insurance should be controversial. Each insurance policy serves a different purpose. You just need to gain enough knowledge to determine which ones are right for you.

Introduction to Insurance Vehicles

Insurance is like a safety net for your finances. It helps protect you from unexpected events that could lead to financial strain or bankruptcy. Understanding the different types of insurance available will help you choose the right one to fit your needs.

Types of Insurance

There are several types of insurance you might consider:

- **Life insurance:** Provides financial support to your loved ones in the event of your passing. Depending on the type of life insurance, you may also be able to borrow cash in an emergency.

- **Health insurance:** Helps cover medical expenses, such as doctor visits and hospital stays.

- **Property insurance:** Protects your home and belongings from damage or theft.

- **Casualty insurance:** Covers liability for accidents or injuries on your property that you may be legally obligated to satisfy.
- **Disability Insurance:** Replaces your income if you become disabled. It is often one of the most overlooked insurances. In my book ***Limitations to Limitless – 7 Proven Strategies To Surviving Disability Without Going Bankrupt***, I outline why this insurance is so critical and how to purchase a good policy. It saved me from bankruptcy after I became disabled several years ago.
- How do you know which one to choose? Don't worry. I've got you covered.

Assessing Insurance Needs

To determine the right insurance for you, consider your financial goals and how much risk you're willing to take. For example, if you have a family depending on your income, life insurance can provide them with financial security if something happens to you.

Here is a scenario with more clarity:

Sarah is a 35-year-old single mother who dreams of owning a second home by the beach. She currently owns a small condo in the city,

which she plans to lease out to help finance her dream.

Sarah's job is stable, but she worries about what would happen if she could not work due to illness or injury.

Sarah's Long-Term Goal:

- Own a second home by the beach for personal enjoyment and potential rental income.

Sarah's Short-Term Goal:

- Save for the down payment on the second home while leasing out her condo.

Sarah's Risk Tolerance:

- Risk tolerance is how much risk you are willing take. We will discuss it much more in-depth in the chapter on investments. Sarah is willing to take a moderate amount of risk to achieve financial security.

Assessing Sarah's needs:

After discussing her situation with her financial coach, **Sarah learns that she needs to consider the following:**

- **Income Protection:** Since Sarah's family depends on her income, long-term disability and life insurance are essential. If Sarah becomes disabled, that income will replace her current income so that her goal is not interrupted. In the event of her passing, life insurance would provide her family with financial security. Sarah opts for a life-term insurance policy that will cover her until her children are financially independent.

- **Property Protection:** Sarah's condo is a valuable asset that she plans to lease out. She needs property and casualty insurance to protect her property. This type of insurance covers damage to the property and provides liability protection in case a tenant or visitor is injured on the premises. Additionally, she explores the option of a separate income protection insurance policy that covers loss of rental income.

- **Savings and Investment:** Sarah decides to put her money in a high-yield savings account and a low-risk investment portfolio to achieve her short-term goal of saving for the down payment on her beach house.

Reflection

Take a moment to reflect on your financial goals and the strategies you've developed to achieve them.

1. **Clarity of Financial Goals:** Have you clearly defined your financial goals? Are they specific and measurable, or are they vague and undefined? Consider whether your goals provide a clear direction for your financial journey. For example, instead of saying, "I want to save money," try setting a specific savings target, like "I want to save $10,000 for a down payment on a house within the next two years."

2. **Alignment with Risk Mitigation Strategies:** Think about the risks that could potentially derail your financial goals, such as job loss, health emergencies, or market fluctuations. Have you considered how to mitigate these risks? Look for ways to align your goals with strategies that provide financial protection. For instance, if your goal is to purchase a rental property, consider what type of insurance you will need.

Key Takeaways

- Building wealth requires a clear action plan, like following a map through an uncharted forest to find hidden treasure.

- An action plan consists of specific, measurable, achievable, relevant, and time-bound (SMART) goals broken down into actionable steps.

- Identifying potential risks, analyzing their likelihood and impact, and prioritizing them are crucial steps in mitigating risks.

- Developing strategies to minimize risks, such as building an emergency fund and getting the right insurance protection, is essential for long-term financial success.

- Setting long-term goals that align with your values and breaking them down into manageable milestones helps you stay motivated and focused.

- Ensuring that your task and risk strategies support your long-term vision and adjusting them as needed are keys to achieving your financial goals.

Now that you have a clear vision and action plan for your financial goals, let's tackle one of the biggest obstacles to financial freedom.

In the next chapter, we'll explore the ins and outs of debt, how it can impact your financial health, and strategies for managing and reducing debt. Whether you're dealing with student loans, credit card debt, or other obligations, understanding how to effectively manage debt is crucial for achieving your financial goals. Let's dive in and start building a solid foundation for a debt-free future.

Key Action

Grab the accompanying workbook or a journal and embark on your goal-setting journey.

Chapter Two

Understanding and Managing Debt

"Debt is the slavery of the free."
—**Publilius Syrus**

Debt. It's a word that can evoke strong and painful emotions for many people. For some, it may bring a sense of dread or anxiety, while for others, it might represent an opportunity or a necessary means to achieve their goals. Regardless of how you feel about it, debt is a financial reality that many of us face at some point in our lives.

Understanding debt, its implications, and how to manage it wisely is crucial for building a secure financial future. In this chapter, we will talk about the different kinds of debt, how they can affect your finances, and ways to manage and get rid of bad debt effectively. If you have student loans, credit card debt, or other debts, this chapter will give you the information and tools you need to get your finances under control.

Types of Debt

Before we dive into strategies for managing and reducing debt, let's first understand the different types of debt you may encounter. Debt can be categorized in various ways. **Here are the most common:**

- **Secure vs. Unsecured Debt**

- - **Secure Debt:** This type of debt is backed by collateral, such as a house or car. If you fail to repay the debt, the lender can seize the collateral to recoup their losses.

  - **Unsecured Debt:** This type of debt is not backed by collateral. Examples include credit card debt and personal loans. Lenders cannot seize your assets if you default.

- **Revolving Debt vs. Installment Debt**

  - **Revolving Debt:** Revolving debt allows you to borrow up to a certain limit, repay the debt, and borrow again. Credit cards are a common form of revolving debt.

  - **Installment Debt:** Installment debt is repaid over time with a set number of scheduled payments. Mortgages and auto loans are examples of installment debt.

- **Fixed-Rate vs. Variable-Rate**

  - **Fixed-Rate Debt:** With fixed-rate debt, the interest rate remains the same throughout the life of the loan, providing predictable monthly payments.

  - **Variable-Rate Debt:** Variable-rate debt has an interest rate that can change over time based on market conditions, leading to fluctuating monthly payments. Be careful of these debts, which can rise significantly when interest rates increase.

- **Short-Term Debt vs. Long-Term Debt**

  - **Short-Term Debt:** Short-term debt is typically repaid within one year. It is often used to cover temporary cash flow needs.

- **Long-Term Debt:** Long-term debt has a repayment period longer than one year. It is commonly used for large purchases like homes or vehicles.

Other types of (consumer) debt that can fall under any of the categories above but are often **treated as standalone categories are**:

- **Credit cards:** These are revolving credit accounts that allow you to borrow money up to a certain limit. They typically have higher interest rates than other types of loans but offer repayment flexibility. They can be short-term or long-term, depending on how long the borrower takes to pay them off.

- **Personal loans:** These are unsecured installment loans that can be used for various purposes, such as debt consolidation, home improvements, or unexpected expenses. They usually have fixed interest rates and repayment terms. They are usually long-term.

- **Mortgages:** A mortgage is a long-term, secured loan used to finance the purchase of a home. Since the property itself serves as security for the loan, the lender may foreclose on the property if you default on your payments.

- **Home equity loans and HELOCs:** These are long-term, secured loans that allow homeowners to borrow against the equity in their homes. Home equity loans provide a lump sum of money with a fixed interest rate, while a home equity line of credit (HELOC) acts as a revolving line of credit with a variable interest rate.

- **Auto loans:** Auto loans are long-term secured loans used to finance the purchase of a vehicle.

- **Student loans:** These loans are designed to help students pay for higher education expenses. They can be federal or private and often have lower interest rates and more flexible repayment options than other types of loans.

Each debt type has its own quirks and repayment strategies. So, stay tuned as we explore ways to tackle them head-on, armed with knowledge and a plan!

Tracking and Identifying All Debts

To effectively manage your debt, you first need to have a clear picture of all your obligations. This includes both secured and unsecured debts, such as mortgages, car loans, credit card balances, and personal loans. **Tracking your debt allows you to:**

- **Understand Your Total Debt:** By listing all your debts, you can see the total amount you owe. This gives you a clearer understanding of your financial situation.

- **Prioritize Repayment:** Once you know how much you owe, you can prioritize which debts to pay off first. High-interest debts or those with unfavorable terms may be the best option if you want to save, but if psychologically you want to have a win, lower balances should be tackled first. We will discuss this in more detail later in the chapter.

- **Identify Outstanding Debts:** Sometimes, debts can be forgotten or overlooked. Tracking your debt ensures you don't miss any payments or incur penalties.

- **Monitor Progress:** As you repay your debts, tracking them allows you to see your progress and stay motivated to continue.

Now, you must put a little work into gathering loan statements. Believe me, you will not regret this. Here are steps that you can follow to track your debt:

Step 1: Gather Your Forces

- **Credit Reports:** These are your financial report cards detailing your credit history and current debt obligations. Grab your free reports from all three major bureaus (Experian, Equifax, and TransUnion) at AnnualCreditReport.com.

- **Statements and Bills:** Collect paper or electronic statements from all your creditors, including credit cards, loans, mortgages, and utilities.

- **Personal Records:** Don't forget debts you might not receive statements for, like medical bills or personal loans from friends or family.

Step 2: Organize the Troops (See workbook exercise)

- **Create a Debt List:** List each debt individually, **including the following:**
    - **Creditor:** The name of the lender or creditor.
    - **Total Amount Owed:** The total amount you owe on the debt.

- Interest Rate: The annual interest rate for the debt.
- Minimum Payment: The minimum monthly payment required.
- Status: Whether the debt is current, delinquent, or in default.

- **Identify Outstanding Debts:** Highlight debts that are past due, have high-interest rates, or are nearing collection. **Add this column to the list above:**
  - **Due Date:** The date by which the payment must be made before it is considered late.

- **Categorize by Type**: Group debts by type (secured, unsecured, revolving, installed, etc.) to understand your overall debt landscape. **This should be another column in your list:**
  - **Type of Debt:** Whether it's a mortgage, car loan, credit card, etc.

Step 3: Intelligence is Key

- **Track Due Dates:** After making the list, mark due dates on your calendar or use a debt management app to avoid missed payments and late fees.
- **Analyze Interest Rates:** Compare interest rates across your debts to identify the ones costing you the most.
- **Calculate Minimum Payments:** Add all your minimum payments to understand your baseline monthly debt obligation.

Once you have this information, you can use it to create a debt repayment plan that fits your budget and helps you achieve your financial goals—let's analyze it further.

Prioritizing Repayment and Utilizing Debt Payoff Strategies

When faced with multiple debts, it's essential to prioritize which ones to pay off first. By strategically focusing on certain debts, you can lower your interest rates, raise your credit score, and reach a state of financial stability faster. **Consider these important strategies when deciding how to pay off your debts in order of importance:**

- **Interest Rates:** Start by paying off debts with the highest interest rates first (debt avalanche method). This approach minimizes the total interest paid overtime.

- **Financial Goals:** Consider your financial goals and how paying off certain debts aligns with them. For example, if you want to buy a home, paying down your high-balance credit card debt can improve your credit score and debt-to-income ratio and reduce your monthly interest payments.

- **Impact on Credit Score**: Delinquent accounts and high credit card balances can negatively impact your credit score. Prioritize debts that are affecting your credit score the most. The utilization rate — which is how much of your available balance is used — has a big impact on your credit score, so the higher the balance, the more it could drag your score down.

- **Tax Implications:** Some types of debt, such as mortgage interest, may be tax-deductible. Consider the tax implications when prioritizing debts.

Bonus Tip: If you have negative credit, you must start doing the work to repair your credit immediately. In my book "*Your Roadmap to 850: The Ultimate 6-Step Guide To A Perfect Credit Score*," you will find practical tips to begin repairing your credit.

Create a Debt Repayment Plan

Two popular methods for paying off debt are the debt avalanche and debt snowball methods. **Here's how they work:**

1. **Debt Avalanche Method:** With this method, you first focus on paying off your debts with the highest interest rates.

    - You first sort the list you made earlier by interest rate, from highest to lowest.
    - Allocate as much money as possible towards the debt with the highest interest rate while making minimum payments on the rest.
    - Once the highest-interest debt is paid off, move on to the debt with the next highest interest rate, and so on.

    Benefits:

    - **Saves Money on Interest:** By focusing on high-interest debts first, you can save money on interest payments over time.

- **Fast Debt Reduction:** Paying off high-interest debts first can lead to faster overall debt reduction.

Drawbacks:

- **Slow Progress at First:** It may take some time to see significant progress on your overall debt balance, especially if your highest-interest debt is also your largest. You may feel discouraged but will see the benefits if you stay the course.

2. **Debt Snowball Method:** The debt snowball method focuses on paying off your smallest debts first, regardless of interest rate.

    - Again, sort your list of debts by balance, from smallest to largest.
    - Allocate extra funds towards paying off the smallest debt while making minimum payments on the rest.
    - Once the smallest debt is paid off, roll the amount you were paying on that debt into the next smallest debt, and so on.

Benefit:

- **Quick Wins:** Paying off smaller debts first can provide a sense of accomplishment and motivation to continue paying off your remaining debts.

Drawback:

- **May Pay More Interest:** By not focusing on high-interest debts first, you may pay more interest over time than you would with the debt avalanche method.

Which method is right for you?

It depends on your personality, goals, and finances. **Consider these factors:**

- **Motivation:** Do you thrive on quick wins or strategic planning?
- **Discipline:** Can you stick to a long-term plan with slower initial progress?
- **Financial literacy:** Are you comfortable tracking interest rates and prioritizing debts strategically?

Ultimately, the best method is the one you'll consistently stick with. When I think about my clients and the path they chose, I would say they have been split down the middle. While I encourage paying less by using the Avalanche method, I see the psychological impact when they pay off a balance, so we work together through the process instead of me prescribing a "right way".

Experiment, track your progress, and choose the approach that keeps you motivated and on the path to debt freedom!

Consolidation and Negotiation with Creditors

I have seen enough to know that just figuring out a repayment plan and sticking to it will not always work from start to finish for everyone; life is full of highs and lows, and low times mean you just might miss out on one or a couple of payments. You can deal with this stress and lessen your financial load by consolidating your debts and negotiating with your creditors.

What is Debt Consolidation?

Debt consolidation is the process of combining multiple debts into a single, more manageable loan. This can be done by taking out a new loan to pay off existing debts or using a balance transfer credit card.

How Does it Work?

With debt consolidation, you take out a new loan or credit card with a lower interest rate than your current debts. This lets you pay off your debts and focus on repaying the new loan or credit card. **Common consolidation options include:**

- **Balance transfer credit cards:** Transfer high-interest credit card balances to a new card with a lower interest rate, often with an introductory period of 0% Annual Percentage Rate (APR).

- **Personal loans:** Take out a personal loan to pay off higher-interest debts, then repay the loan with a lower interest rate.

- **Home equity loans or lines of credit:** Use the equity in your home to consolidate debts. These typically offer lower interest rates but require your home as collateral.

Benefits of Debt Consolidation:

- **Simplified Repayment:** Instead of managing multiple debts and due dates, you only have one payment to cover each month.

- **Lower Interest Rates:** If you can secure a lower interest rate with your consolidation loan or credit card, you may save money on interest over time.

- **Improved Credit Score:** Consolidating your debts can potentially improve your credit score by reducing your overall debt load and making it easier to manage payments.

Drawbacks of Debt Consolidation:

- **Risk of Accumulating More Debt:** Consolidating your debts doesn't address the underlying issues that led to the debt. Without changing your spending habits, you may end up accumulating more debt. I have seen this happen to those who have not worked on their mindset.

- **Fees and Costs:** Some consolidation loans or balance transfer credit cards may come with fees, which can add to the overall consolidation cost.

- **Impact on Credit Score:** Opening a new credit account for consolidation can temporarily lower your credit score.

Best Situation to Use:

Debt consolidation is best suited for individuals with multiple high-interest debts who are committed to changing their spending habits, can qualify for a lower interest rate, and are disciplined enough to avoid getting into additional debt.

What is Negotiation with Creditors?

Negotiation with creditors involves contacting your creditors to discuss your financial situation and agreeing on new terms for repayment. This can include lower interest rates, reduced monthly payments, or even a settlement for less than the full amount owed.

How Does it Work?

- **Contact Your Creditors:** To negotiate with creditors, you'll need to contact them directly and explain your financial difficulties. You can then propose a new repayment plan that is more manageable for you. This is where you could switch from either of the plans (avalanche or snowball) to the one that suits you more.

- **Offer a Lump Sum Payment:** If you can afford it, offer to settle the debt for a lump sum payment that is less than the total amount owed. Creditors may accept this to avoid the risk of not receiving any payment.

- **Seek Professional Help:** Consider working with a credit counseling agency or financial coach. The credit counseling agency will negotiate with your creditors on your behalf and help you develop a plan to repay your debts. Be careful of credit counseling agencies requesting high upfront payment and instead identify a nonprofit one. With the help of a financial coach, you can learn the skills you need to handle your money on your own. You can not only use what you know but also teach others.

Benefits of Negotiation with Creditors:

- **Reduced Debt Burden:** Negotiating with creditors can result in lower monthly payments or a reduced overall debt amount, making it easier for you to repay your debts.

- **Avoidance of Bankruptcy:** Negotiating with creditors can help you avoid bankruptcy, which will negatively affect your credit score.

- **Improved Financial Situation:** By negotiating new terms with your creditors, you can improve your financial situation and avoid further financial hardship.

A Drawback of Negotiation with Creditors:

- **Time and Effort:** Negotiating with creditors can be time-consuming and may require you to provide detailed financial information.

Should You Negotiate?

Negotiation with creditors is best suited for individuals who are experiencing temporary financial difficulties and want to avoid more serious consequences, such as bankruptcy.

Note: Reductions offered by creditors will have tax implications, so be sure to speak with your tax advisor

Debt Relief Companies

Unlike debt consolidation, these companies will help you to pay off your debt by negotiating with select creditors on your behalf. You do not make any payment on the debt during this negotiation period. Instead, you save your money to make payments once an agreement is reached. While debt relief may sound good, and there may be reputable companies that can skillfully negotiate on your behalf, **I will caution you about going this route because of the following concerns:**

- **Ruined Credit:** since you are no longer paying on your debt, your credit will begin to get ruined once you are 30 days past due.

- **High Fees:** These companies make money from the fees they charge you, which can be significant.
- **Taxes:** If you receive a relief, you will likely be taxed.
- **Legal Action:** Companies could decide not to negotiate with you and instead file a lawsuit against you.

I had a client with stellar credit and quite a few unsecured debts. She became disabled and went to a debt relief company. Upon reviewing the contract that she was about to sign; they were charging her over $14,000 on less than $80,000 total debt. Some debts were not being negotiated with creditors, and because they had advised her to stop making payments, her credit was ruined. I worked with her to negotiate the debt on her own and began working with her to rebuild her credit and tweak her budget so that she could work on fulfilling the negotiated payment amounts.

Improving Credit and Building a Strong Credit Score

Understand Your Credit Score

What is a Credit Score? Your credit score is a three-digit number that represents your creditworthiness based on your credit history.

How is it Calculated? Factors such as payment history, amounts owed, length of credit history, new credit, and types of credit used influence your credit score.

Ways to Improve Your Credit Score

- **Pay Bills on Time:** Ensure you pay all bills, including credit card bills, on time.

- **Reduce Debt:** Work on reducing your overall debt, especially credit card balances.

- **Keep Credit Utilization Low:** Try to keep your credit card balances below 30% of your credit limit. If your credit is blemished, the utilization should be as low as 7%.

- **Don't Close Old Accounts:** Keeping old accounts open can help improve your credit history length.

- **Regularly Check Your Credit Report:** Monitor your credit report for errors and address any issues promptly.

Building a Strong Credit History

- **Apply for a Secured Credit Card:** A secured credit card can help you build credit if you have little or no credit history.

- **Become an Authorized User:** Being added as an authorized user on someone else's credit card can help you establish credit.

- **Apply for a Credit Builder Loan:** These loans are designed to help you build credit by making small monthly payments.

Benefits of a Strong Credit Score

- **Lower Interest Rates:** A strong credit score can qualify you for lower interest rates on loans and credit cards.

- **Easier Approval for Loans:** Lenders are more likely to approve your loan applications with a strong credit history.

- **Better Insurance Rates:** Some insurance companies use credit scores to determine rates, so a higher score can lead to lower premiums.

Improving and maintaining a strong credit score is crucial for your financial health. To get better financial opportunities in the future, it is important to be responsible with your debt and build a good credit history. So, hang in there and stay on course.

Reflection

- Take a moment to reflect on how your current debt situation is affecting your financial goals. Are there ways in which your debts are holding you back from achieving your dreams? Consider how reducing or eliminating your debt could open new possibilities for your future. Make a list and keep track of your debts, choose a plan, and don't give up.

- Imagine the satisfaction of progressing towards your goals, just like with a bucket list, proudly ticking off one debt after the other. Each step towards debt freedom brings you closer to financial security and the ability to pursue your passions without the burden of debt weighing you down.

Key Takeaways

- Debt is a common financial reality that many people face at some point in their lives, and understanding how to manage it is crucial for building a secure financial future.

- There are different types of debt, including secure, unsecured, revolving, installment, fixed-rate, variable-rate, short-term, long-term, and consumer debts.

- Tracking all your debts and identifying outstanding debts is essential for effective debt management.

- Prioritizing repayment and utilizing debt payoff strategies, such as the debt avalanche and snowball methods, can help you pay off debt more efficiently.

- Consolidation and negotiation with creditors are strategies that can help manage debt during difficult times.

- Improving credit and building a strong credit score is key for long-term financial health.

Having tackled the complexities of debt management, you're now equipped to shift your focus toward establishing lasting financial security. In the following chapter, we delve into the intricacies of retirement planning, emphasizing the importance of a retirement plan and maximizing contributions. We also investigate investment fundamentals, helping you define your investment goals, understand investment principles, and learn how to invest wisely.

Additionally, we discuss the significance of diversity in investments and guide you through creating a diversified portfolio. In no time, you'll be well on your way to securing your financial future and achieving your long-term goals. See you there!

Chapter Three

Establishing Financial Security

> *"Financial security is not a dream. It's a priority that requires hard work, discipline, and most importantly, a plan."*
> **—Rob Berger**

Have you ever felt the weight of financial uncertainty? Wondering if you'll ever stabilize everything? I know that feeling all too well. It's like standing at the base of a mountain and staring up at the summit, unsure of the path ahead. But just as every mountain is conquered step by step, financial security can be achieved, one careful decision at a time.

We must focus on long-term planning while we continue to work on short and medium-term goals.

In this chapter, we'll cover the practical steps you can take to set up a retirement plan, define your investment goals, and embrace the diversity of investments, all to create a stable and secure financial future. So, let's lace up our boots, take one step at a time, and ascend toward the summit of financial security together.

Retirement Plans and Maximizing Contributions

It's a mouthful, I know. You might be wondering why we are talking about retirement so early in the book. It was a deliberate decision, because this is one of the easiest ways for you to save. And, because too many people are not saving for retirement.

If you already have a retirement plan, that is excellent! You are on the right path. If you don't, no worries; It is never too late to start. I will guide you on how to start.

What is a retirement plan, and why do you need one?

As the popular saying goes...If you fail to plan, you plan to fail.

The expected outcome of any event or experience determines the way you plan for it. When it comes to financial security, your planning starts with the end in mind. This is where a retirement plan comes in. It serves as a roadmap for your future, guiding you on saving and investing money now to enjoy financial security later in life.

The goal of the retirement plan is to ensure that you have enough money to support yourself when you leave the workforce -- providing tranquility and a comfortable lifestyle in your golden years. **Having a solid retirement plan is important because it helps you:**

- Save enough for retirement.
- Cover expenses like healthcare and housing.
- Maintain your lifestyle after you stop working.
- Enjoy your retirement years without financial stress.

So, whether you dream of traveling the world or simply spending more time with your loved ones, a solid retirement plan is the key to making those dreams a reality.

First, we'll discuss how to start a good retirement plan. Then, we will talk about how to keep (or change, if necessary) a plan that is already in place.

The Right Way To Start A Retirement Plan

If you have made the decision to start a retirement plan, but you are feeling anxious and overwhelmed, primarily because you cannot afford to get it wrong or you just don't know where to start. **Here are some key things you need to know about a retirement plan before you start:**

You can create a retirement plan through your employer or open an individual retirement account (IRA). The most important requirement for an IRA, is that you have earned income such as your salary and bonus from a job, income from self-employment, or commission. **There are two types of IRAs:**

- **Traditional IRA**: Contributions are made to your account before taxes (if your income is below a certain threshold). There is a mandatory date on which you must begin to make withdrawals. If you do not withdraw by that date, you will receive a penalty. Once you begin withdrawing from your IRA, you will be taxed.

- **Roth IRA**: Contributions to this account are made with after-tax dollars. Unlike the traditional IRA, you will not be eligible for an annual tax deduction, but one of the unique advantages is that once you withdraw your money, you will not be taxed. Another great advantage is that you can withdraw your money at any time once you reach the retirement age without any penalties.

It is important that weigh the pros and cons to decide which one makes the most sense for your situation. For example, if you think you will be in a higher tax bracket when you retire, the better option may the Roth IRA. This is a simplistic answer, however, because we would need to better understand your long terms goals and current and future plans to more accurately make that decision.

Both types of IRAs can be opened through a broker such as Charles Schwab or Fidelity, or even using an app like Stash. By working with a financial coach or advisor you can decide what types of account to open and the types of investments to put in your account.

1. **Eligibility and Options:**

   - Are you eligible? Check if your employer offers a retirement plan like a 401(k) or 403(b) and if you meet their eligibility criteria (e.g., minimum work hours). Call your human resources office to learn more.

   - **Explore your options:** If you're eligible for an employer-sponsored plan, compare it to an IRA. Consider factors like contribution limits, fees, and investment choices.

     o **Contribution Limits:** Understand the maximum that you can contribute to your retirement plan or to an IRA annually. These limits change annually, so stay updated.

     o **Understanding Fees:** Different plans and investment options within plans have varying fees. Common fees include expense ratios, management fees, and other charges which reduces the overall growth of your investment.

2. **Investment Basics:**

   - **Define your goals:** What are you aiming for in retirement? Consider factors like desired lifestyle, age, and expected expenses.

   - **Investment types:** Understand the different asset classes, such as stocks, bonds, and cash, and how risky each one is. You will need to know how much risk you are willing to take and base your investment decision on that.

   - **Diversification:** This is the process of investing in different types of assets. For example, stocks, bonds, or funds, to spread your risk.

3. **Risk Tolerance:** What is your comfort level with risks? For example, ask yourself. If I invest in this asset, will I become stressed out worrying that I may lose all my money?

4. **Choosing Investments:**

   - **Self-directed options:** If you choose individual investments, research thoroughly and consider seeking professional advice.

   - **Target-date funds:** If you want to set it and forget it, consider target-date funds. They automatically adjust the assets that you own as you approach retirement. You must understand the benefits and limitations of these types of funds.

(We discuss much more about investing in the later sections of this chapter and later in the book.)

5. **Staying Informed:**

   - **Stay up-to-date:** Keep yourself informed about changes in tax contribution limits, tax laws, and investment strategies.

   - **Review regularly:** Regularly review your retirement plan and portfolio, adjusting as needed based on your goals and life changes.

6. **Additional Tips:**

   - **Start early:** The earlier you start contributing to your retirement plan, the more time your money has to grow through compounding interest. I began at age 22 and had over a million by age 48.

   - **Seek professional help:** If you feel unsure, consider seeking guidance from a financial coach.

Everything in the list above gets you one foot through the door as it takes care of the general knowledge that everyone should know. Your situation is unique to you and requires special attention. Now, let's get you completely through the door and well seated.

To emphasize how everyone's financial situation is different, I'll use a real-world scenario to demonstrate how to tailor this approach to specific circumstances.

David's Roadmap to Retirement Riches: Planning Starts Now!

David, a 30-year-old marketer, envisions a perfect retirement, complete with various homes and luxurious travels. He has explored whether to take advantage of the 401(k) plan that his employer offers or to use a Traditional or Roth IRA.

Current Scenario:

- **Age:** 30
- **Retirement Goal:** Age 65 (35 years away)
- **Desired Lifestyle:** Multiple houses, frequent vacations

Step 1: Choose a Retirement Account:

Since he can contribute substantially more under his employer's 401(k) plan, and his employer matches the first 3% of his contribution, he decides to put his retirement in the 401(k) plan.

How does David decide? He likes the benefits of the traditional IRA because it allows him to make his own investment decisions and contribute before taxes. However, he still weighs the option of using the Roth IRA since contributions are made with after-tax dollars. He likes the idea that he will not have to pay taxes once he begins to withdraw during his retirement.

He, however, realizes that he will be limited in how much he can contribute if he uses the traditional IRA or Roth IRA. Therefore, he would not be able to grow his retirement as fast as he would like. He also realizes that he can take advantage of the 3% that his employer is matching.

He ultimately decides to contribute to his employer's 401(k) plan.

Step 2: Set a Contribution Goal:

David's aim is to accumulate over $3 million by the time he retires at 65. With 35 years to achieve his goal, he has committed to contributing $20,000 annually, estimating an annual return of 8%, resulting in a monthly contribution of $1,667.

Step 3: Calculate Investment Returns:

David plans to invest in a diversified portfolio of stocks and bonds, aiming for an average annual return of 8%. He uses a compound interest calculator to see how his investment grows over time.

Here's David's Optimized Plan:

David sets up automatic monthly contributions of $1,667 to be deducted from his employer. Assuming an average annual return of 8% on his entire portfolio, he regularly monitors his progress and adjusts his contributions as needed to stay on track toward his $3 million goal.

For simplicity, we will assume that David earns the expected 8% annually. When David reaches 65, he will have an excess of $3.5 million in his retirement plan since this calculation only includes his contribution and not the 3% contributed by his employer.

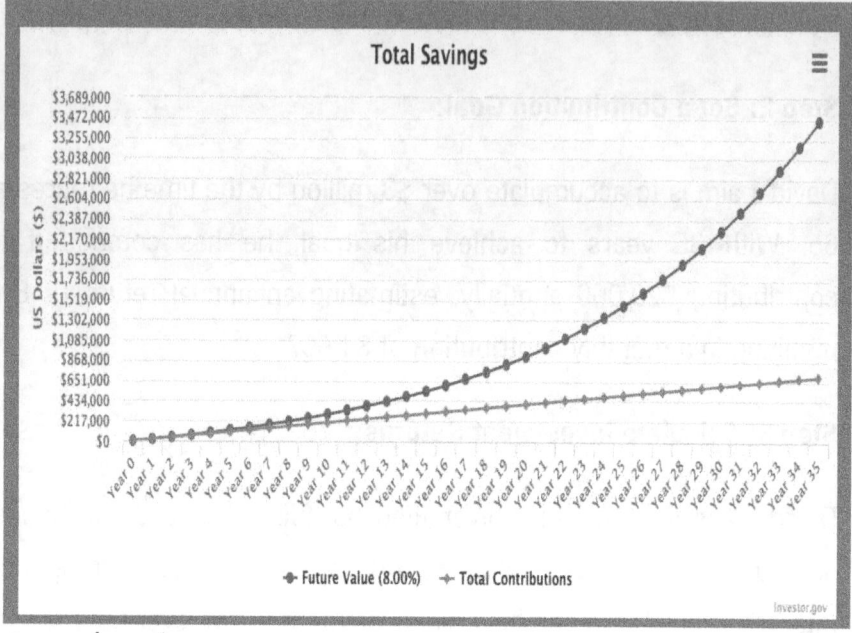

Source: *Investor.gov*

Doing it right

Here are some common mistakes people make in retirement planning and **how you can avoid them:**

1. **Underestimating the cost of retirement:**
   - **Mistake:** Assuming current expenses will translate directly to retirement.
   - **Do it right:** Remember that prices will increase over time, so be sure to factor in inflation, healthcare costs, and potential lifestyle changes. While this will vary based on several factors, a good projection may be 70-80% of current income.

2. **Starting too late:**
   - **Mistake:** Procrastinating and thinking you have plenty of time later.

- **Do it right:** Start saving as early as possible. Thanks to the power of compounding, even small contributions will grow over time. If David decided to wait until he was 35 to start investing and invested $24,000 every year, he would only have $2.7 million. While this is still great, his retirement is almost $1 million less.

3. **Not saving enough:**

    - **Mistake:** Contributing only the minimum or relying solely on Social Security.

    - **Do it right:** Determine your target retirement goal and contribute consistently to reach it. Max out employer-sponsored plans and utilize IRAs, Roth IRAs, and Healthcare Savings Accounts (HSA).

4. **Investing too conservatively:**

    - **Mistake:** Focusing solely on low-risk investments with minimal returns.

    - **Do it right:** Diversify your portfolio across different types of assets, such as stocks, bonds, and real estate, to balance risk and potential rewards. Consider your age and risk tolerance when making investment decisions.

5. **Ignoring taxes:**

    - **Mistake:** Neglecting to factor in taxes on withdrawals from certain retirement accounts.

    - **Do it right:** Understand the tax implications of different retirement plans and choose options that align with your tax goals. Consider Roth IRAs for tax-free withdrawals in retirement.

6. **Not rebalancing your portfolio:**

    - **Mistake:** Setting it and forgetting it, leading to too many of the same assets in your portfolio over time.

    - **Do it right:** Review your portfolio regularly and sell some investments if needed. You would then replace those investments with new investments in different industries or sectors. This could help you to maintain your desired asset allocation and risk profile.

7. **Neglecting health insurance:**

    - **Mistake:** Assuming Medicare will cover all healthcare costs in retirement.

    - **Do it right:** Healthcare cost is one of the largest expenses during retirement. Research supplemental insurance options to cover gaps in your coverage and budget for potential healthcare expenses. If you are eligible to set up a Healthcare Savings Account, you should. The contributions and withdrawals are tax-free as long as they are used for healthcare costs.

8. **Not planning for long-term care:**

    - **Mistake:** Ignoring the possibility of needing assisted living or nursing home care in the future.

    - **Do it right:** Research long-term care options and consider long-term care insurance or other financial strategies to cover potential costs. Many insurance companies have stopped offering stand-alone long-term care policies and instead offer them as riders to another policy. If you are unable to get a reasonably priced policy, you will need to identify other financial strategies to cover potential costs.

9. **Not having an estate plan:**

    - **Mistake:** Leaving your assets and wishes unclear leads to potential legal issues and complications for your loved ones.

    - **Do it right:** Create a will, power of attorney, and other necessary documents to ensure your wishes are followed after your passing.

10. **Not seeking professional advice:**

    - **Mistake:** Feeling overwhelmed and navigating retirement planning alone.

    - **Do it right:** Consider consulting with a financial coach who can help you to personalize a plan based on your unique circumstances and goals.

If you already have a retirement plan, then here is how you can ensure that it will allow you to comfortably live your life free of worry.

1. **Evaluate your current plan:**

    - **Understand your contribution amount:** How much are you currently contributing, and does it align with your goals?

    - **Check fees and expenses:** Look into any fees associated with your plan and see if more cost-effective options exist.

2. **Re-evaluate your retirement goals:**

   - **Have your goals changed?** Do you envision a different lifestyle in retirement or have new expenses to consider?

   - **Adjust your target retirement age:** Do you want to retire earlier or later? This will affect your savings needs.

   - **Calculate your estimated retirement income:** Consider social security, pensions, and other sources besides your retirement plan.

3. **Increase contributions if possible:**

   - **Aim for consistency:** Even small increases over time can significantly impact your final nest egg.

   - **Maximize employer contributions:** Take advantage of any employer matching programs.

   - **Explore additional saving options:** Consider traditional or Roth IRAs, side hustles, or other investment opportunities.

4. **Regularly rebalance your portfolio:**

   - **Maintain your desired asset allocation:** Rebalance as needed to account for market fluctuations and your evolving risk tolerance.

   - **Stay diversified:** Keep your portfolio spread across different asset classes to manage risk and optimize returns.

5. **Stay informed and adapt:**

   - **Keep up with financial news and market trends:** Monitor your investments and be prepared to adjust your strategy when necessary.

- **Seek professional advice:** Consider consulting a financial coach for personalized guidance and ensure your plan remains on track.

- **Review your plan at least annually:** Adjust your contributions, allocations, and overall strategy as needed.

Bonus Tip: Retirement planning is a marathon, not a sprint, and while you want to have the financial resources, it involves so much more. Consider developing hobbies, social connections, and activities you enjoy, ensuring a fulfilling and happy retirement beyond finances.

Quick question: Did you notice a recurring core factor at the heart of retirement planning? Did you guess it right? **It's Investment(s).**

Regular contributions, even when made at the maximum level for any individual plan, if invested in very low-yielding investments, can only go so far and accumulate to barely or just enough to get by comfortably. Developing a plan that matches your risk tolerance, which we will discuss later, will help you to grow your retirement, as David did in the example we discussed. Do not make the mistake of leaving your investment in a low interest rate fixed account because it will never be enough.

I have a client who is still in her thirties. More than 70% of her account was in a fixed account, earning less than 5%. Ultimately, she moved some of the money out, but if she continues at the same pace, she will not have enough in retirement.

Investments can make or break your retirement plan. Hence, it's a crucial factor that cannot be overemphasized. The next section will explore the ins and outs of investment to equip you for success.

I deliberately chose to discuss retirement in the early part of the book because it is one of the biggest goals that most people have not planned for. A report by Bloomberg several years ago showed that most people worldwide are unprepared for retirement. In America, almost half the population is not.

Defining Investment Goals and Understanding Investment Principles

By now, you must have an action plan that follows the SMART principle. If you don't, please pause here, grab the accompanying workbook, take some time, and create one. This is how you really start moving things forward. By taking actionable steps!

Understanding Investment Principles:

Investing can seem complex, **but it boils down to a few principles:**

- **Risk and Return:** Generally, higher returns come with higher risk. You need to understand your risk tolerance.

- **Diversification:** Don't put all your eggs in one basket. Diversifying your investments can help manage risk.

- **Time Horizon:** The longer your investment horizon, the more risk you can afford to take.

- **Costs and Fees:** Be aware of the costs associated with your investments, as they can eat into your returns (i.e. how much you will earn on your investment) over time.

- **Stay Informed:** Stay updated on market trends and economic indicators that can affect your investments.

This is but a brief introduction which will be addressed in greater detail in a later chapter.

Learning to Invest and Research Investment Options

Learning about investing and researching options can be daunting, but it's achievable! **Here are some steps and resources to get you started:**

1. **Identify your learning style:**

    - Do you prefer structured learning? Consider online courses offered by financial coaches like myself or platforms like Coursera.

    - Enjoy hands-on learning? Explore investing simulators or "paper trading" platforms to practice investing without real money.

    - Learn best through interactive experiences. Attend workshops or webinars hosted by financial coaches, institutions, or investment firms.

    - Need more hands-on help? Work in small groups or one-on-one with a financial coach who will guide you through the process.

A note about Financial Coaches and Financial Advisors: Financial coaches educate you on how to manage your money and develop investment and risk management strategies. You have the power to ask the right questions and make educated decisions about your finances. The role of financial advisors is to manage the money you have. Many are not interested in providing any education and will not meet with you if your money is below a certain dollar threshold.

2. **Research specific investment options:**

- Once you grasp the basics, delve deeper into different asset classes: stocks, bonds, mutual funds, ETFs, real estate, etc. Understand their characteristics, risks, and potential returns.

- **Analyze individual companies or funds:** Start with well-established, reputable companies or broad-market index funds for initial research. Use credible financial websites like Yahoo Finance or Google Finance to access company data and analyst reports.

- **Read investment news and commentary:** Stay informed about market trends and economic news, but be wary of hype and short-term predictions.

Embracing Diversity in Investments:

Diversity is not just a buzzword; it's a fundamental principle of investing. Spreading your risk across different asset classes, industries, and regions of the world is what a diversified portfolio does. This makes your investments less vulnerable to changes in the market. Embracing diversity means not putting all your eggs in one basket. It is more about building a portfolio that can handle changes in the market.

Creating a Diversified Portfolio:

To create a diversified portfolio, **consider the following key points:**

- **Asset Allocation:** Determine the right mix of asset classes (stocks, bonds, cash, and real estate) based on your risk tolerance and investment goals.

- **Industry and Sector Diversification:** Invest in companies across different industries – healthcare, finance, manufacturing to reduce the risk in your investment portfolio if the economy goes south.

- **Global Diversification:** Consider investments in international countries to reduce the risk of being too reliant on one country's economy.

- **Rebalancing:** Regularly review and rebalance your portfolio to maintain your desired asset allocation.

Benefits of a Diversified Portfolio:

- **Risk Management:** Diversification reduces the impact of a single investment's poor performance on your portfolio.

- **Stability:** A diversified portfolio is more stable and can provide more consistent returns over time.

- **Opportunity for Growth:** By investing in different assets, you can take advantage of growth opportunities in various sectors and markets.

Creating a diversified portfolio requires careful planning and ongoing management. By embracing diversity in your investments, you can build a stronger, more resilient portfolio that helps you achieve your financial goals.

Reflection

A retirement plan is one of the easiest and most important ways that we can begin saving for our future. There are various options to choose from, and each one should be evaluated separately to determine the best option for you.

Consider annual contribution limits, fees and taxes when deciding on a plan, and weigh the different investment options.

You should periodically revisit your plan to ensure that it is in line with your goals and objectives.

Key Takeaways

- **Retirement Planning:** A retirement planning roadmap is crucial for financial security, providing a roadmap to save and invest for a comfortable retirement. Starting early and understanding contribution limits, fees, and investment basics are key factors in creating a successful retirement plan.

- **Investment Principles:** Understanding key investment principles like risk and return, diversification, time horizon, and costs can help you make smart investment decisions and manage risk effectively.

- **Learning to Invest:** Building a strong knowledge foundation through free online resources, books, podcasts, and YouTube channels can help you understand investing basics and research specific investment options effectively.

- **Diversified Portfolio:** Embracing diversity in investments is crucial for managing risk and optimizing returns. A diversified portfolio spreads risk across different asset classes, industries, and regions, reducing the impact of volatility on your investments.

- **Benefits of Diversification:** A diversified portfolio provides risk management, stability, and growth opportunities. Regularly review and rebalance your portfolio to maintain your desired asset allocation and achieve your financial goals.

In addition to establishing financial security, another critical component to success is your mindset! Just like an athlete needs mental toughness to win the game, you need a positive and powerful outlook to conquer your financial goals.

In the next chapter, we will discuss how to develop a winner's mindset, overcome negative thoughts, and stay motivated on your path to financial freedom. Get ready to unlock your inner champion and smash those financial targets!

Chapter Four

Cultivating A Mindset for Success

"Growing wealth is never about how much you make. It is always about how you use what you make, and it starts with your budget."
—Tanya Taylor

Do you ever find yourself wanting to achieve something big – a dream vacation or maybe a major investment – but then self-doubt creeps in? You start wondering if you're really capable or if you deserve it.

This is where cultivating a mindset for success comes into play. It's about establishing the beliefs, attitudes, and habits that will help you confidently face obstacles and reach your big goals. Consider this: two people with similar incomes and expenses. One struggles to make ends meet, living paycheck to paycheck, while the other effortlessly builds wealth and achieves financial freedom. What's the difference? It's all in how they think about money.

This chapter will explore the psychology of money and how changing your mindset helps you achieve financial freedom. We will also talk about common mindset blocks that keep people from reaching their financial goals and give you ways to develop a mindset of abundance and success. Are you ready to change your thoughts about money and your financial future?

The Psychology of Money and How Our Mindset Affects Financial Decisions

Imagine you're at the store, craving a treat. You see a fancy chocolate bar for $5, but your usual one is $2. You might think, "Five bucks is way too much!" That's the psychology of money in action—your money mindset. It's like a voice whispering ideas about money, like how much to spend or save.

This voice can be helpful, but sometimes it can hold you back. Maybe you tell yourself, "I can't afford to save," even if you could put away a little each week. This fear of spending or saving too much is called a scarcity mindset. It can make you feel like you never have enough money, even if you do.

On the other hand, an abundance mindset is believing there's always more money to be made and saved. It encourages you to think about the future and make choices to help you reach your goals, like saving for a vacation or a new car.

So, the next time you're faced with a financial decision, pay attention to that voice in your head. Is it telling you to be scared of spending or saving? Push those ideas to the side and pick the path that will help you reach your long-term goals. Always keep in mind that your mindset can be your friend, not your enemy, when it comes to money.

Common Mindset Blocks To Financial Success And How To Overcome Them

Many common mental blocks can get in the way of your financial success. **Here are a few important ones and how to deal with them:**

1. **Scarcity Mindset:**

   - **Block**: As we have seen above, you believe there's never enough money, leading to feelings of fear and deprivation.

   - **Example**: You avoid budgeting because it feels restrictive, or you constantly worry about running out of money.

   - **Overcome**: Shift to an **abundance mindset**. Focus on what you have and ways to **grow** your wealth. Practice gratitude for your current resources and visualize your financial goals to fuel motivation.

2. **Fear of Failure:**

   - **Block**: The fear of losing money or not achieving financial goals paralyzes you from taking any action.

   - **Example**: You avoid investing or starting a side hustle because you're afraid of losing money, even though your decision could be ten times your wealth.

   - **Overcome**: Acknowledge the fear, but don't let it control you. **Start small** and celebrate your progress. Seek **education and guidance** to build your confidence in making sound financial decisions.

3. **Imposter Syndrome:**

    - **Block**: You feel like you don't deserve financial success or lack the skills to manage your money effectively.

    - **Example**: You compare yourself to others who seem financially savvy and feel incapable of achieving the same measure of success.

    - **Overcome**: Recognize that everyone starts somewhere. Focus on **learning and improving** your financial knowledge. Surround yourself with **positive influences** who support your financial goals and celebrate your achievements.

4. **Procrastination:**

    - **Block**: Due to laziness or fear, you constantly put off important financial decisions or actions, like creating a budget or repairing your credit.

    - **Example**: You keep saying you'll "start tomorrow" but never actually take any concrete steps toward your financial goals.

    - **Overcome**: Break down large tasks into **smaller, manageable steps**. Set **realistic** deadlines and reward yourself for completing them. Utilize **tools and apps** that automate your finances, making the process easier.

5. **Living in the "Now":**

    - **Block**: You prioritize instant gratification over long-term financial planning, leading to impulsive spending and neglecting future goals.

    - **Example**: You prioritize expensive experiences or purchases over saving for retirement or important milestones.

- **Overcome**: Visualize **your future desires** and the financial security you want to achieve. Remind yourself of the **long-term benefits** of responsible spending and saving.

Strategies For Cultivating A Mindset Of Abundance And Financial Empowerment

The Strategies for cultivating a mindset of abundance and financial empowerment involve reforming your thinking patterns and adopting new habits. **Here are some actionable steps you can take:**

- **Practice Gratitude Daily:** Start each day by writing down three things you're grateful for. This simple practice helps shift your focus from scarcity to abundance, reminding you of the positives in your life.

- **Set Clear Financial Goals:** This is a reminder that setting clear financial goals is a crucial part of the big picture, and doing it right puts you steps forward in your wealth-building journey. I am happy to point out that you would have already done this if you had been doing the action items. If not, grab the **workbook** and get started now.

- **Visualize Your Financial Success:** Spend a few minutes each day visualizing yourself achieving your financial goals. Imagine how it will feel to be debt-free, have a fully funded emergency fund, or reach your retirement savings target. This practice helps reinforce positive beliefs and motivates you to take action.

- **Practice Mindful Spending:** Before making a purchase, pause and ask yourself if it aligns with your financial goals.

Consider whether the item will truly bring you lasting satisfaction or if it's a temporary fix for a deeper issue. This practice helps you become more intentional with your money, avoiding impulse purchases.

- **Surround Yourself with Positive Influences:** Engage with people with a healthy attitude towards money and financial success. Share your goals with supportive friends or join online communities such as my Grow Your Wealth Facebook and Instagram Community, which is focused on financial empowerment. Surrounding yourself with positivity can help reinforce your mindset shifts.

- **Educate Yourself Regularly:** Take time out each day to learn something new about personal finance. This could be reading a finance-related article, listening to a podcast, or watching a video. Continuous learning helps build your financial knowledge and confidence.

- **Celebrate Your Financial Wins:** Acknowledge and celebrate your progress, no matter how small. This could be reaching a savings milestone, sticking to your monthly budget, or paying off a debt. Celebrating your wins reinforces positive behavior and encourages you to keep going.

The Role Of Visualization And Affirmations In Goal Setting And Achieving Financial Success

We cannot speak about mindset without clarifying the connection between the mind and external influences that can shape it. These influences are the things we see and words we say to ourselves, hence, visualization and affirmation.

Now, people can say many things to you and even see through patterns of experience, but ultimately, what you visualize and affirm to yourself is what affects and defines the outcome of your financial endeavors.

Visualization and affirmations are powerful tools that can help you achieve your financial goals by harnessing the power of your mind. **Here's how they work:**

Visualization: Seeing is Believing

What it is: Visualization is the practice of creating vivid mental images of yourself already achieving your financial goals. Imagine yourself debt-free, owning your dream home, or traveling the world.

How visualization helps

- **Motivation boost:** Visualizing success keeps you focused and inspired to keep pushing forward.
- **Problem-solving:** It allows you to anticipate challenges and plan ways to overcome them in advance.
- **Brain training:** Your brain starts to believe what you visualize, aligning your actions with your goals.

Affirmations: Words Shape Reality

What they are: Affirmations are positive statements that you repeat to yourself, focusing on what you want to achieve financially. For example, "I am worthy of financial abundance" or "I am a money magnet."

How affirmations help

- **Change your beliefs:** Affirmations help you replace negative money beliefs with positive ones.

- **Boost confidence:** They help you to start believing in yourself and feel capable of achieving your goals.

- **Focus on positivity:** Affirmations keep you centered on your goals, even when obstacles arise.

How to Use Them

- **Be specific:** Don't just visualize "becoming wealthy," focus on a specific goal, like the exact amount you want to save.

- **Make it vivid:** Use all your senses, and imagine how you'll feel and act when you achieve your financial goal.

- **Daily practice:** Repeat your affirmations and visualize your goals regularly; morning and night are great times.

- **Believe it:** Don't just recite words; truly believe in what you're visualizing and affirming.

Visualization and affirmations are not extraordinary tools. They are most effective when combined with action and the development of good financial habits. However, they are great tools for improving your thinking and propelling you toward your financial goals.

Organizing Financial Documents and Establishing a Filing System

Are you wondering how your mindset and having a tidy filing system work together to support your financial journey? **Cultivating a mindset for success and organizing your financial documents are deeply connected in several ways:**

1. **Clarity and Control:** A success mindset often emphasizes clarity and control over different aspects of life. This extends to your finances. Having a well-organized system for your financial and other important documents provides financial clarity, allowing you to see your income, expenses, debts, and investments all in one place. This clarity empowers you to make informed financial decisions and track progress toward your goals.

2. **Reduced Stress and Improved Focus:** A cluttered financial life can be stressful and overwhelming. Constantly searching for documents or worrying about losing them can distract and hinder your focus. By organizing your finances, you reduce unnecessary stress and free up mental space to focus on your financial goals and other important areas of your life. This improved focus allows you to make strategic financial decisions and implement your plans more effectively.

3. **Increased Efficiency and Time Management:** A success mindset prioritizes efficiency and time management. When your financial documents are organized, you can easily find the information you need, saving valuable time and effort. This efficiency allows you to complete financial tasks quickly and easily, freeing up

time to pursue other financial opportunities or simply relax, knowing everything is in order.

4. **Building Positive Habits and Confidence:** Cultivating a success mindset involves building positive habits that support your goals. By taking the initiative to organize your finances, you are setting a positive precedent for yourself. This consistency and follow-through build confidence in your ability to manage your finances effectively, further propelling you towards achieving your financial goals.

5. **Fosters a Sense of Responsibility and Accountability:** A success mindset emphasizes taking responsibility and being accountable for your actions. Organizing your financial documents reflects a sense of responsibility toward your financial well-being. Having everything organized demonstrates your commitment to managing your finances diligently.

Building a success mindset and organizing your finances go hand-in-hand, creating a powerful synergy that empowers you to take charge, reduce stress, make informed choices, and ultimately reach your financial goals.

Tips for organizing financial documents, including using digital tools and systems

Let's face it, financial documents can feel like a tangled mess. Just the idea of gathering documents from very different sources can be highly discouraging. Here are some tips to help you establish a filing system that works for you and helps you stay organized, **leveraging both traditional and digital tools:**

1. **Declutter and Categorize:** Set aside a few hours 2 or 3 days during the week – add it to your calendar.

    - **Identify by category:** Bills, investments, taxes, insurance, etc. Select one category to work on during the blocked-out timeslot.

    - **Gather all your documents:** Statements, receipts, tax forms, etc. Repeat the process until you have gathered all the documents.

    - **Discard unnecessary documents:** Shred or recycle expired papers securely.

2. **Embrace Digital Solutions:**

    - **Scan important documents:** Use a scanner or scanner app to digitize paper copies.

    - **Utilize online storage platforms:** Cloud storage services offer secure document storage and access from various devices.

    - **Use budgeting and finance apps:** These apps can help you track income, expenses, and investments, reducing reliance on physical documents. Visit our website at growyourwealth10x.com to download a complimentary guide on budgeting and finance apps.

3. **Create a Digital Filing System:**

    - **Organize folders within your chosen platform:** Mirror the categories you used for physical documents.

- **Name folders clearly and concisely:** Use keywords that make them easily identifiable.

- **Sub-categorize if needed:** if you have many categories, create subfolders for further organization.

4. **Automate When Possible:**

   - **Set up paperless statements:** Request electronic versions of bills and statements from providers.

   - **Enable auto-pay for recurring bills:** This reduces the risk of missed payments and saves time.

   - **Utilize automatic document filing:** Some apps can automatically categorize and file scanned documents based on keywords.

5. **Schedule Regular Reviews:**

   - **Dedicate time for document review:** Semi-annually or at least once per year is recommended.

   - **Delete outdated documents:** Shred physical copies after establishing a secure digital backup.

   - **Update information and track progress:** Review your financial health and adjust your strategy as needed.

Bonus Tips:

- **Label physical documents clearly:** If you choose to keep physical copies, label them clearly for easy identification.

- **Utilize color coding:** Assign different colors to different categories for visual organization.

- **Back up your digital files:** Regularly backup your digital documents to an external drive or cloud storage for added security.

- **Get a fireproof safe:** Store all important documents, such as birth and marriage certificates, in a fireproof, waterproof safe.

Reflecting on Achievements and Adjusting Goals as Necessary

As I have said earlier, your financial journey is like a marathon, not a sprint. While staying focused on the finish line is important, it's equally crucial to pause and reflect along the way. Reflecting on your achievements and adjusting goals as needed is a vital practice for sustained success.

Why reflect?

Taking time to reflect offers multiple benefits:

- **Reinforces Positive Habits:** Celebrating your wins, even small ones, reminds you of the good financial decisions you've made. This creates a positive feedback loop, encouraging you to keep up the good work.

- **Boosts Motivation:** Reflecting on past successes reminds you of your potential and what you can achieve. This fuels your motivation to continue working towards your financial goals, especially when you face challenges, and trust me, you will face many challenges and setbacks along the way.

- **Builds Confidence:** Acknowledging your progress, no matter how small, builds your financial confidence. It helps you believe in managing your money effectively and overcoming obstacles.

- **Identify Areas For Improvement:** Reflecting on your successes also allows you to identify strategies that have worked well. You can then replicate these strategies to achieve even greater financial success in the future.

- **Promotes Gratitude:** Taking time to appreciate your financial achievements cultivates a sense of gratitude. This positive mindset can attract more abundance and reduce financial anxiety.

How to Reflect

- **Schedule regular reviews:** Dedicate time (weekly, monthly, or quarterly) to reviewing your financial situation. You decide the pace, but I recommend you schedule it and be consistent, so that it eventually becomes automatic. To begin, I recommend weekly reviews.

- **Track your progress:** Use a journal, spreadsheet, or budgeting app to track your spending, savings, and progress toward debt reduction or investment goals.

- **Ask yourself questions:**
    - What milestones have I achieved?
    - What challenges did I overcome?
    - Are my current goals still relevant?

        - Are there areas where I can improve?
        - Do I need to add new goals?
    - **Be honest and objective:** Don't sugarcoat your progress or ignore potential shortcomings. Honest reflection allows for meaningful course corrections; otherwise, lying to yourself will eventually lead to stagnation, or you will quit.
    - A former client came into my coaching programs excited about fixing her finances and moving towards building wealth. I recommended that she build a budget and monitor it over a period, which she did and was doing a great job.Then life happened, and she hit some roadblocks. She would report that things were going well each time, but it was obvious that it was not. I began working with her to identify ways in which she can reroute. Still, it was so difficult for her to accept that she would need to make adjustments that instead of sticking it out, she disappeared and never responded to any communication. I am not sure where she is today, but I know that with a few tweaks, she could have continued her wealth-building path. I am afraid she just gave up and is back to being stuck. I encourage you to stay the course no matter how tough it gets.

Adjusting Goals

Sometimes, reflecting reveals the need to adjust your goals. This is not a sign of failure but rather a sign of growth and adaptability. **Here are some scenarios:**

- **Life circumstances change:** Job loss, unexpected expenses, or family changes might necessitate adjusting your budget or timelines.

- **Goals no longer resonate:** You might discover your priorities or interests have shifted, requiring adjustments to your financial aspirations.

- **Identified areas for improvement:** Reflection might reveal areas where your original goals lacked ambition or weren't specific enough.

Important Note: Adjusting goals is not about giving up; it's about fine-tuning your strategy for long-term success. It's about constantly reassessing your financial landscape and making informed decisions to ensure your journey aligns with your evolving needs and aspirations.

If you consistently reflect on and adjust, you will stay grounded, remain motivated, and ensure your financial journey leads you toward a fulfilling and secure future.

Reflection

- Take a moment to think about how you can feel more positive about money and your financial future. Consider small changes you can make to be more optimistic about your finances.

- Are there any negative thoughts or beliefs about money holding you back? Try to replace them with positive affirmations. Also, visualize yourself achieving your financial goals regularly to boost motivation and confidence.

Key Takeaways

- Cultivating a mindset for success is essential for achieving financial goals, as it influences how you think about and manage money.

- Your mindset can either hinder or propel you towards financial success, so it's important to address common mindset blocks like scarcity mindset, fear of failure, imposter syndrome, procrastination, and living in the moment.

- Strategies for cultivating a mindset of abundance and financial empowerment include practicing gratitude, setting clear financial goals, visualizing success, practicing mindful spending, surrounding yourself with positive influences, educating yourself regularly, and celebrating your financial wins.

- Visualization and affirmations are powerful tools that can help you achieve your financial goals by harnessing the power of your mind.

- Organizing your financial documents and establishing a filing system is crucial for maintaining clarity, reducing stress, improving focus, increasing efficiency, and building positive financial habits.

- Reflecting on your achievements and adjusting your goals as necessary is a vital practice for sustained financial success, helping you reinforce positive habits, boost motivation, build confidence, identify areas for improvement, promote gratitude, and ensure your financial journey aligns with your evolving needs and aspirations.

Ready to put your newfound mindset into action? Head over to the workbook to put your success plan into action. The next chapter aims to show you how to master budgeting and harness good spending habits. Building on your understanding of financial psychology, we'll discuss practical strategies to manage your money effectively and reach your financial goals faster.

Part Two

Implementing Effective Financial Strategies

"Financial strategy is the bridge between your dreams and your destination. Build it wisely, and you'll cross with confidence."

Chapter Five

Mastering Budgeting and Spending Habits

"Do not save what is left after spending, but spend what is left after saving."
—Warren Buffett

Let's say you finally land your dream vacation - a week on a pristine beach with crystal-clear water and swaying palm trees. You have been planning for months, with every detail of the itinerary nailed down. You finally get to your destination. You are about to pay for your beachfront villa when your card gets declined!

Uh oh! What happened?

This scenario highlights the crucial role of budgeting and managing spending habits in achieving financial success. Without a plan, even the most well-intentioned dreams can turn into stressful situations.

Why is this so important? Just like building a sturdy house, a secure financial future requires a solid foundation. **Budgeting and managing spending habits act as one leg of this foundation, providing:**

- **Clarity:** Knowing exactly where your money goes empowers you to make informed decisions about your finances.

- **Control:** Taking charge of your spending allows you to prioritize your goals and allocate resources accordingly, reducing the need to get into excessive debt.

- **Peace of mind:** Budgeting helps avoid unexpected financial burdens and fosters a sense of security.

- **Progress towards goals:** By managing your spending, you free up resources to save and invest, bringing you closer to your financial aspirations.

Think of it like this: even the most determined traveler might get lost without a map. Budgeting is your financial map, guiding you toward your financial destination.

Tracking All Your Spending and Identifying Areas for Improvement

Have you ever experienced the sinking feeling of a declined card at checkout? It's a situation that can leave anyone feeling embarrassed and frustrated. But imagine if you could rewind time and prevent this scenario altogether.

Wouldn't you want to track your spending meticulously to understand what led to that situation? By recording and categorizing them by priority, you could identify areas for improvement. This knowledge empowers you to make informed financial decisions in the present, ensuring similar moments don't occur in the future.

Besides saving you from public embarrassment, tracking your finances has benefits you cannot overlook. **Here's a concise overview** of the benefits of tracking your spending and how it empowers better financial decision-making:

The Advantages of Tracking Your Spending

- **Illuminates your spending patterns:** Where does your money actually go? Tracking expenses brings clarity, often revealing areas where you unknowingly overspend.

- **Identifies "money leaks":** Small, seemingly harmless purchases can add up. Think about your daily coffee, barely used subscriptions, or dining out frequently. Tracking expenses pinpoints these leaks so you can plug them.

- **Aligns spending with values:** Does your expenditures support what truly matters to you? Tracking spending encourages you to assess whether your money genuinely serves your goals and priorities.

- **Reduces financial anxiety:** Gaining control of where your money goes brings this feeling of calmness and stability and reduces stress related to your financial situation.

- **Creates accountability:** Tracking spending makes you answerable for every purchase, promoting mindful spending and discouraging impulse buys.

How Tracking Leads to Better Financial Decisions

- **Informed budgeting:** Accurate spending data gives you a realistic basis for creating a budget that reflects your spending habits and helps you reach your goals.

- **Targeted savings:** Knowing where you can cut back allows you to allocate more funds towards savings, accelerating your progress toward financial milestones.

- **Strategic debt payoff:** Tracking expenses highlights areas where you can save money and put those savings towards eliminating debt faster.

- **Prioritized purchases:** Before swiping your card, you can pause and ask yourself, "Does this align with my goals?" This simple question prevents impulsive spending and ensures your money works for you.

- **Empowered investor:** By freeing up funds through better spending habits, you open doors to intelligent investments to build long-term wealth.

Tools and methods for tracking spending

- **Embrace the Digital Age:**
    - **Budgeting Apps:** Popular options like Mint, YNAB, and Rocket Money offer convenient ways to track income expenses and categorize transactions. They can even automate data entry through bank integrations and set spending goals. Grab your free guide at growyourwealth10x.com
    - **Financial Tracking Websites:** Websites like NerdWallet offer free budgeting tools and resources to help you track your spending and manage your finances.

- **Go Old School:**

- **Spreadsheets:** Create a customized spreadsheet using tools like Microsoft Excel or Google Sheets. This allows for flexibility and control over your data but requires manual entry. Visit my site at growyourwealth10x.com for a simple Excel spreadsheet to start your budgeting immediately.

- **Pen and Paper:** Track your expenses in a notebook or personal finance journal. This method offers portability and can be a good starting point, but it can be time-consuming to analyze data, and if it gets lost, it will be a big setback.

Choosing the Right Tool:

Consider your preferences and needs. If you value convenience and automation, an app might be ideal. If you prefer customization and control, a spreadsheet might be better. If you are not tech-savvy and need pen and paper, then grab one that works for you. The bottom line is to not let these small decisions stand in the way of your big goal.

More Tips:

- **Utilize statements and receipts:** These provide a detailed record of your transactions and spending habits.

- **Set realistic goals:** Aim for consistency and track your spending regularly, even if it's just weekly or bi-weekly.

Identifying Areas for Improvement

Once you have a system in place, **it's time to analyze your data and identify areas for improvement:**

1. **Categorize your expenses:** Group your spending into categories like groceries, bills, entertainment, and transportation. This helps identify areas where you might be overspending.

2. **Review spending trends:** Look for patterns or recurring expenses that might seem unnecessary or excessive. For example, frequent dining out or impulse purchases at the grocery store.

3. **Compare your spending to your income:** Analyze where your income goes and ensure essential expenses like rent or utilities are prioritized within budget.

4. **Evaluate your priorities:** Use your spending data to assess if your expenses align with your financial goals. Are you spending heavily on things that don't truly matter long-term?

5. **Be honest with yourself:** Don't shy away from difficult truths. Acknowledging areas where you can cut back is crucial for progress.

6. **Don't go it alone:** If you believe you cannot do it, get a financial coach like me to help you. Not only will you be motivated, but you will also be held accountable.

Combining effective tracking tools and critical analysis of your spending data will give you valuable insights into your financial habits and identify areas for improvement, paving the way for smarter financial decisions and a brighter financial future.

In a way, keeping track of your spending is like turning on a spotlight on your money. You get more attention, more power, and the chance to build a safe future on your own terms. But that's not all; there's another team player who is—budgeting.

Creating a Budget or Spending Plan Based on Income and Expenses

Managing your money effectively often starts with an important step right after putting down a tracking system: creating a spending plan or budget. While these terms are sometimes used interchangeably, they offer subtle differences, and choosing the right one can benefit your financial journey.

Budgeting: A Structured Approach

A traditional budget is a predetermined allocation of your income towards different spending categories like housing, transportation, food, and savings. It often involves setting specific, fixed amounts for each category and tracking your spending against them. **This approach is ideal for:**

- **Individuals seeking precise control:** If you crave a structured framework for managing your finances, a budget provides clear guidelines and limitations.

- **Debt repayment:** Budgets are highly effective for individuals prioritizing debt repayment, as they allow for allocating specific amounts towards debt each month.

- **Saving for specific goals:** Whether it's a dream vacation or a down payment on a house, a budget ensures you save consistently towards your goals.

Spending Plan: A Flexible Framework

A spending plan offers a more flexible approach to managing your finances. While it still involves tracking income and expenses, the focus is on prioritizing goals and allocating resources accordingly. **This approach is best suited for:**

- **Individuals comfortable with a less rigid method:** If you prefer flexibility and room for adjustments, a spending plan allows for more autonomy.

- **Individuals with fluctuating incomes:** If your income varies month-to-month, a spending plan allows you to adjust allocations accordingly.

- **Those seeking a balance between structure and flexibility:** A spending plan offers a middle ground between a strict budget and completely free spending. It provides a framework for your finances while allowing for unexpected expenses or occasional treats.

Choosing the Right Approach

The ideal approach depends on your circumstances and preferences. A budget is the path forward if you crave a structured framework and detailed control. If you value flexibility and a goal-oriented approach, a spending plan might be more suitable.

Creating Your Plan or Budget

Here are the steps to create either a spending plan or budget, **with some key differences highlighted:**

1. **Gather your financial information:**

Mastering Budgeting and Spending Habits

- Collect your income statements, bank statements, and any existing statements which show your monthly spending. Don't forget receipts if paid for with cash.

2. **Calculate your net income:**

- This is your take-home pay after taxes and deductions.

3. **Track your expenses (highly recommended):**

- For a budget, track your expenses for a specific period (e.g., 2- 3 months) to understand your spending patterns.

- For a spending plan, you can utilize existing knowledge of your spending habits.

4. **Categorize your expenses:**

- You should have already done this exercise when you identified areas for improvement above.

5. **Choose your preferred method:**

- **Budget:**
  - Use the 50/30/20 rule (50% needs, 30% wants, 20% savings/debt repayment) as a starting point.
  - Allocate specific amounts to each spending category based on your needs, goals, and past spending (if tracked).

- **Spending plan:**
  - Review your income and spending categories.
  - Identify areas where you can realistically cut back or redirect funds toward your goals.

- Prioritize your expenses, ensuring essential needs are met before allocating funds for other categories.

6. **Track your progress regularly:**

- Monitor your spending and adjust your plan or budget as needed. This is crucial for both approaches.

Remember:

- **Be realistic:** Set realistic goals and expectations based on your income and lifestyle.
- **Be flexible:** Your plan or budget can evolve over time as your circumstances and goals change.
- **Stay motivated:** Celebrate your progress and reward yourself for achieving milestones.

Ultimately, both methods empower you to:

- Gain control over your finances.
- Make informed spending decisions.
- Work towards achieving your financial goals.

Managing Spending Effectively and Adjusting Your Budget as Needed

Creating a budget or spending plan is just half a step. Sticking to it and adapting it as your financial situation evolves will set you up for long-term stability and success. **Here are some tactics to manage your spending effectively and adjust your budget with flexibility:**

- **Mastering Spending Strategies:**

  - **Embrace the cash envelope system:** Allocate specific amounts of cash for different spending categories (groceries, entertainment, etc.) and use them throughout the month. Seeing your money physically dwindle can deter unnecessary spending. This will require you to always have physical cash and pose a higher risk of loss.

  - **Utilize automatic transfers:** Set up automatic transfers for essential expenses like rent and utilities. This ensures bills are paid on time and removes the temptation to spend that designated money.

  - **Leverage technology:** Budgeting apps provide tools to track spending, set spending goals, and receive alerts when nearing limits. Consider utilizing these features to stay mindful of your spending habits.

  - **Embrace the "pay yourself first" approach:** Allocate at least 10% of your income towards savings, or you will always find something to spend it on.

- **Adapting Your Budget for Change:** Life is dynamic, and your budget should be too. **Anticipate and adjust your plan as your financial circumstances evolve:**

  - **Income Changes:** Did you receive a raise or experience a pay cut? Adjust your income portion in your budget accordingly. If you receive a raise, consider increasing your savings or debt repayment allocations rather than significantly increasing your spending.

- **Unexpected Expenses:** Life throws curveballs. Prepare for them by including a cushion in your budget or spending plan to handle unforeseen expenses like car repairs or medical bills.
- **Shifting Priorities:** As your life goals change, re-evaluate your spending priorities. Perhaps you're saving for a wedding or planning a family vacation. Adapt your budget to accommodate these evolving priorities by creating sinking funds.

- **Flexibility is Key:** A rigid budget can become restrictive and lead to discouragement. **Embrace flexibility within your plan:**

  - **The 50/30/20 Rule:** Remember this rule? It provides a starting point but should be adjusted based on your individual circumstances.
  - **Review Regularly:** Don't set your plan in stone. Regularly review your spending habits and income stream, adjusting as needed. This will ensure your budget remains relevant and effective.

There's no "one size fits all" approach. Experiment with different strategies and find what works best for you and your financial situation.

Strategies for Saving and Investing Surplus Funds

Creating a successful financial plan goes beyond just managing your income and expenses. It's crucial to develop strategies for saving and investing any surplus funds you have after covering essential expenses and debt obligations.

The Power of Saving and Investing:

Saving and investing your surplus funds offer numerous benefits:

- **Building Wealth:** Over time, your savings and investments can grow through compound interest, enabling you to accumulate wealth and achieve your long-term financial goals like retirement or a comfortable lifestyle.

- **Financial Security:** Building an emergency fund can provide a safety net for unexpected expenses like car repairs or disability, preventing financial hardship.

- **Achieving Financial Goals:** Whether you're saving for a dream vacation, a down payment on a house, or securing your child's education, saving, and investing can help you reach your financial aspirations.

The Art of Saving:

Effective savings involves strategic planning and discipline:

- **Establishing an Emergency Fund:** Aim to save 3-6 months of living expenses to cover unexpected emergencies and avoid going into debt. Your budget or spending plan is your guide to how much you spend monthly.

- **Setting Specific Goals:** Identify your short-term and long-term goals (e.g., new car, college fund) and allocate specific savings towards each. Utilize different savings accounts for different goals, making them less readily accessible for impulse spending.

- **Automating Savings:** Set up automatic transfers from your paycheck into your savings account. This "pay yourself first" approach ensures consistent savings and removes the temptation to spend that money.

Investing for Growth:

Once you've established a solid financial foundation with your emergency fund and targeted savings, consider investing your surplus funds for potential long-term growth. You can jump two chapters back to chapter three for a revision on how to get started with setting up a retirement plan and learning how to invest. Chapter eight provides a deeper dive into the nuances of investment.

Reflections

- Are your spending habits aligned with your financial goals? Take a moment to consider whether your current spending habits are helping or hindering your progress toward your financial goals. Are you spending in line with your priorities and values? For example, if your goal is to save for a house, but you find yourself spending a significant portion of your income on dining out or shopping, it may be time to reevaluate your priorities and adjust your spending habits.
- How can you make adjustments to your budget to achieve better financial outcomes? Start by reviewing your current budget and identifying areas where you can cut back or

reallocate funds towards your financial goals. This could involve reducing discretionary spending, such as eating out less frequently or finding more affordable alternatives for your regular expenses. Additionally, consider setting specific savings goals and automating your savings to ensure you're consistently putting money towards your goals. By making small, manageable adjustments to your budget, you can start to see improvements in your financial situation and move closer to achieving your long-term goals.

Key Takeaways

- Budgeting and managing spending habits are essential for financial success, providing clarity, control, peace of mind, and progress toward goals.

- Tracking spending helps identify patterns and leaks, align spending with values, reduce financial anxiety, and create accountability.

- Effective tracking tools include budgeting apps, financial tracking websites, spreadsheets, and pen-and-paper methods.

- Creating a budget or spending plan involves gathering financial information, calculating net income, tracking expenses, categorizing expenses, and choosing a preferred method.

- Budgeting offers structured control, ideal for debt repayment and saving for specific goals, while a spending plan offers flexibility, making it suitable for fluctuating incomes.

- Managing spending effectively involves embracing strategies like the cash envelope system, automatic transfers, leveraging technology, and paying yourself first.

- Adapting your budget for change requires anticipating and adjusting to income changes, unexpected expenses, shifting priorities, and embracing flexibility.

- Saving and investing surplus funds are crucial for building wealth, financial security, and achieving financial goals.

- Effective saving involves establishing an emergency fund, setting specific goals, and automating savings while investing for growth can be considered once a solid financial foundation is established.

Do you ever imagine facing a financial emergency only to discover you're woefully unprepared? Don't let that happen! The next chapter delves into the essentials of building an emergency fund, your financial safety net for life's unexpected storms. Buckle up and learn how to create a buffer that protects your dreams while weathering any financial downpour.

Chapter Six

Building an Emergency Fund

*"Expect the best. Prepare for the worst.
Capitalize on what comes."*
—Zig Ziglar

It's Friday night, and you're halfway through ordering takeout when your phone rings. It's the car mechanic, and the news isn't good. Your car needs a major repair, costing more than you have readily available. Panic sets in – how will you handle this unexpected expense? Unfortunately, this scenario is all too familiar for many people who haven't built an emergency fund.

What if you didn't need to lose your peace? Could you smile and say to yourself, "I saw this coming?" or simply shrug it off and order your food?

Remember the buffer of funds (from budgeting) I asked you to allocate for unexpected expenses? That's your emergency fund; it's a financial shield that protects your sanity, comfort, and overall well-being — yeah, the unexpected can drive you crazy and even make you sick just trying to process it.

An emergency fund is a dedicated pool of savings specifically designed to cover unforeseen expenses like car repairs, medical bills, or sudden job loss.

Why You Need an Emergency Fund:

- **Avoid Debt:** Unexpected expenses won't force you to rely on high-interest credit cards.

- **Reduce Stress:** Knowing you have a safety net eases financial anxieties.

- **Maintain peace-of-mind:** You can face challenges with security and confidence, knowing you have resources to cover essentials.

- **Financial Security:** Protects your savings goals and covers unforeseen expenses like car repairs or medical bills.

Difference Between Emergency Funds and Other Savings Accounts

Yes, there are differences, and knowing just how different an emergency fund is from other savings accounts will hugely impact what role it plays in your financial journey. While both emergency funds and other savings accounts involve setting aside money, **they have distinct purposes, priorities, and accessibility levels:**

- **Emergency Funds:**
    - **Purpose:** Serve as a safety net to cover unexpected expenses like car repairs, medical bills, or sudden job loss.
    - **Priority:** Establishing an emergency fund should be a top priority for financial stability.

- **Accessibility:** The funds should be easily accessible and liquid, meaning readily available for withdrawal without penalties. Savings accounts and money market accounts are suitable options.

- **Interest Rate:** Depending on the balance in your emergency fund, you may still be able to earn interest. However, you must prioritize availability over maximizing returns. You can consider a high-yield savings or money market account.

• **Other Savings Accounts – Sinking funds:**

- **Purpose:** Funds that cater to specific financial goals, such as a down payment on houses or cars or even a vacation.

- **Priority:** The priority for contributing to these accounts varies depending on your individual goals and financial situation.

- **Accessibility:** Unless these are goals for 2-5 years, you should keep your balance in a liquid account, or there may be restrictions on withdrawals, such as penalties for early withdrawal.

- **Interest Rate:** Typically offer higher interest rates as compared to emergency funds as they prioritize long-term growth over immediate accessibility. **Examples include:**

  - **Certificates of Deposit (CDs):** Offer guaranteed returns but lock your money away for a fixed term, typically with penalties for early withdrawal.

In summary:

- Emergency funds are for immediate needs and prioritize accessibility over high returns.

- Sinking fund accounts may be for short or long-term goals. Depending on how far into the future you will need these funds, you can choose to put the money in either a high yield savings account, a money market account, or a CD, if interest rates are good.

Building Your Emergency Fund: Starting Strong with What You Have

The journey towards financial security begins with critical self-assessment. Before embarking on the path to building your emergency fund, evaluating your current financial situation and existing savings is important. This foundational step provides a clear understanding of your starting point and empowers you to set realistic goals for building your financial safety net.

Taking Stock:

- Go back to the previous step where you created your budget or spending plan.

Honesty and Awareness:

This initial assessment might have revealed areas for improvement. Don't be discouraged by any initial discoveries; consider them stepping stones towards a more secure future. It is crucial to approach this entire process with honesty and awareness.

Setting Realistic Goals:

With a clear picture of your current financial situation, it's time to **set realistic and achievable goals for building your emergency fund:**

- **Emergency Fund Size:** While a 3-6 month worth of living expenses is often recommended, a smaller, attainable goal can be an excellent starting point. Aim for $500 or $1,000 initially, and gradually increase your target as your financial situation improves.

- **Funding Plan:** Based on your newly created or revised budget/spending plan, how much can you allocate towards this fund? Based on that amount, determine how long it will take to save the 3-6 months and add that to your goals, which you will monitor and adjust when necessary.

- **Utilize Existing Savings:** If you have any existing savings, consider reallocating a portion towards your emergency fund. This jumpstart can significantly boost your progress and motivate you to continue saving.

Tips to Manage Expenses Without Tapping Your Emergency Fund: Facing the Unexpected

Life throws curveballs, and sometimes expenses arise when you least expect them. While an emergency fund is essential, it's equally important to know how to navigate unexpected costs without draining your financial safety net. **Here are some practical tips to help you manage:**

1. **Prioritize and Evaluate:**

- **Assess the urgency:** Determine if the expense is truly urgent or can be temporarily delayed. For example, a car repair might be essential for daily transportation, while a new phone purchase can likely wait.

- **Evaluate alternatives:** Explore options to address the situation without a significant financial impact. For a one-time fix, could you borrow a tool instead of buying one? Can the expense be negotiated or split into smaller payments?

2. **Utilize Available Resources:**

   - **Tap into existing savings:** If you have dedicated savings goals besides your emergency fund, consider temporarily borrowing a small amount to cover the unexpected expense. Remember to replenish these savings as soon as possible.

   - **Sell unused items:** Do you have unused electronics, clothes, or furniture in good condition? Selling them online or through a garage sale can generate quick cash to cover the expense.

   - **Seek alternative income sources:** Consider taking on a short-term side hustle like freelancing, dog walking, or participating in online surveys. This can generate additional income to address the unexpected cost without dipping into your emergency fund.

   - **Rental Income:** If you own your home and find an unused basement or room, consider renting it out for a period that will allow you to build your emergency fund.

3. **Communicate and Negotiate:**

   - **Communicate with creditors:** If you're facing difficulty managing a bill, be proactive and communicate with the creditor. Explain your situation and explore options like payment plans or temporary adjustments. Open communication can often lead to flexible solutions.

   - **Negotiate prices:** Don't be afraid to negotiate, especially for non-essential goods or services. This could involve negotiating a lower repair cost, seeking discounts, or exploring alternative service providers with potentially lower rates.

4. **Temporary Lifestyle Adjustments:**

   - **Reduce discretionary spending:** Temporarily cut back on non-essential expenses like entertainment, dining out, or subscriptions you rarely use. This frees up funds to address the unexpected cost without impacting your long-term savings goals.

   - **Meal prep and cook at home:** Eating out frequently can significantly impact your budget. Consider preparing meals at home for a more cost-effective option.

   - **Utilize free or low-cost alternatives:** Look for free or low-cost alternatives for entertainment, hobbies, or transportation. Explore libraries, parks, community events, or public transportation instead of relying solely on paid options.

Always remember to:

- **Be transparent with yourself:** Be honest about your financial situation and avoid taking on additional debt unless necessary.

- **Prioritize long-term goals:** While addressing unexpected expenses is important, don't jeopardize your long-term financial goals by depleting your savings.

- **Seek guidance if needed:** Don't hesitates to seek help from a financial coach or credit counselor if you need assistance navigating a challenging financial situation.

Revisiting and Adjusting: Why Your Emergency Fund Needs to Evolve

Building a robust emergency fund is crucial for financial security, but it's a journey, not a destination. As your life and circumstances change, so should your emergency fund goals. Regularly reviewing and adjusting your fund size ensures it continues to serve its purpose effectively.

Why Revisiting and Adjusting Your Emergency Fund is Essential.

1. **Changing Needs:**
   - **Life stage transitions:** Your financial needs evolve as you progress through life stages. A young adult starting their

career might need a smaller emergency fund compared to a family with children or individuals nearing retirement.

- **Increased expenses:** As your income grows, your standard of living likely changes, impacting your emergency fund needs. For example, a larger home might translate to higher potential maintenance costs, requiring a larger emergency buffer.

- **Improve your credit:** A good credit score allows for more flexibility and options for lower interest rate debt, which means you will be paying out less monthly on debt that you are carrying. Grab a copy of my book, *"Your Roadmap to 850: The Ultimate 6-Step Guide To A Perfect Credit Score,"* and start repairing your credit today.

- **Debt repayment:** Successfully paying down debt frees up income you can allocate towards increasing your emergency fund to a more comfortable level.

2. **Inflation's Impact:**

    - **Purchasing power:** Over time, inflation erodes the purchasing power of your money. Regularly reviewing your emergency fund size ensures it maintains its power to cover unexpected expenses in the face of rising costs.

3. **Job Security Changes:**

    - **Career shifts:** Entering a new field with potentially less job security might necessitate a larger emergency fund to provide a safety net during potential job transitions.

Benefits of Reviewing and Adjusting

- **Boost confidence:** Knowing your emergency fund is adequately sized for your current needs reduces financial anxiety and provides a sense of security, ultimately boosting your confidence when going about your daily life.

- **Financial flexibility:** Aligning your emergency fund with your current needs allows you to allocate your resources more effectively towards other financial goals like saving for retirement or a down payment on a house.

- **Efficient resource allocation:** Avoiding an unnecessarily large emergency fund frees up resources that can be invested or used toward other financial goals with potentially higher returns.

How to Review and Adjust

- **Evaluate your current situation:** Assess your income, expenses, debt obligations, and life stage.

- **Review your financial goals:** Consider your short- and long-term financial aspirations.

- **Research cost estimates:** Research average costs for potential emergencies relevant to your current situation.

- **Calculate an updated target:** Based on your evaluation and research, determine an updated target amount for your emergency fund.

- **Adjust your saving strategy:** Increase or decrease your savings contributions as necessary to reach your new target. If you decrease your target, you should put that money towards investing in one of your other long-term goals.

Common Challenges in Building an Emergency Fund and How to Address Them

Building an emergency fund is essential for financial security, but let's be honest: it's not always easy. Many obstacles can stand in your way, making it difficult to consistently save and reach your goal. But fear not, for every roadblock, there's a solution:

Reflection

- Do you have sufficient emergency funds to cover unexpected expenses?

    - Have you ever found yourself in a situation where an unexpected expense caught you off guard, and you wished you had a financial safety net?

    - How would having a robust emergency fund change your approach to handling unexpected financial challenges?

- What steps can you take to build and maintain a robust emergency fund?

- Are there areas in your budget where you could cut back or save more to contribute to your emergency fund?

- How can you prioritize building your emergency fund in your financial planning, even if your current budget feels tight?

Key Takeaways

- Building an emergency fund is crucial for financial stability and peace of mind, providing a safety net for unexpected expenses.

- An emergency fund helps avoid debt, reduces stress, maintains peace of mind, and ensures financial security by covering unforeseen expenses.

- Differentiate between emergency funds and other savings accounts, understanding their purposes, priorities, and accessibility levels.

- Start strong with what you have by evaluating your current financial situation, setting realistic goals, and utilizing existing savings to jumpstart your emergency fund.

- Manage expenses without tapping into your emergency fund by prioritizing and evaluating expenses, utilizing available resources, and temporarily adjusting your lifestyle.

- Regularly revisit and adjust your emergency fund to align with changing needs, inflation, job security changes, and financial goals.

- Address common challenges in building an emergency fund by staying committed, prioritizing savings, automating contributions, and seeking support when needed.

Many people dream of being financially free and stable despite the hectic pace of everyday life. We've talked about making a budget, saving money, and setting up an emergency fund. But what about making more money? Imagine being able to follow your dreams, travel, or save for the future without having to worry about money all the time. In the next chapter, we'll uncover strategies for boosting your income and exploring entrepreneurship, opening doors to new opportunities and financial growth.

Chapter Seven

Increased Income and Entrepreneurship

> *"Don't be afraid to give up the good to go for the great."*
> **—John D. Rockefeller**

Increasing income and entrepreneurship are important for wealth accumulation and a better life, but they play different roles. Let's imagine two friends, Grace and Jenny.

Grace – The Steady Climber

Grace works hard at her job and gets regular promotions. Her income increases steadily over time. **This allows her to:**

- **Cover her basic needs and expenses:** She can afford rent, food, transportation, and utilities comfortably.

- **Save for the future:** With a higher income, Grace can set aside more money each month. This builds her emergency fund and allows her to invest for retirement or a down payment on a house.

- **Enjoy a good standard of living:** Grace can afford some luxuries beyond basic needs. She might travel occasionally, eat out at nice restaurants, or pursue hobbies she enjoys.

Jenny – The Entrepreneur

Jenny decides to take a risk and start her own business. It's challenging. At first, and her income fluctuates. However, after a few years, her business takes off. **This allows her to:**

Increased Income and Entrepreneurship

- **Potentially earn significantly more:** Entrepreneurs have the potential to 10x their wealth at a much quicker pace than traditional jobs, but it comes with risk.

- **Be her own boss:** Jenny has more control over her work schedule and direction.

- **Innovation and Impact:** She can create something new and solve problems in her immediate community and globally.

Building Wealth Together

Both Grace and Jenny are on a path to wealth accumulation. Grace's steady income and money management habits allow her to save consistently, while Jenny's business has the potential for high profit if successful. **They can both use their increased income to:**

- **Invest:** Growing their money over time through stocks, bonds, real estate, or other investment vehicles.

- **Pay off debt:** Paying down debt and reducing interest payments frees up more money for saving and investing.

- **Enjoy Life:** Living and enjoying life in the now should also be a part of your goals.

Entrepreneurship isn't for everyone — not everybody has the boldness for it — but it offers the potential for higher rewards. A stable income allows for consistent savings. Both approaches can lead to financial security and a better quality of life. Whether you have a stable, promising job or are an entrepreneur, at the end of the day, you generate income that will support your life and dreams. But what is the connection between income and financial stability?

Scenario: Saving for a House

Let's say both Grace and Jenny want to buy a house. Grace, with her stable income, might qualify for a traditional mortgage with a regular down payment. With her less consistent income from the business, Jenny might need to save a larger down payment or wait for her business to establish a track record of profitability.

The Relationship Between Income and Financial Stability

Income and financial stability have a strong positive relationship. In simpler terms, higher income, if managed effectively, will lead to greater financial stability. **Here's why:**

- **Meeting basic needs:** A comfortable income allows you to cover essential expenses like housing, food, and transportation. This reduces financial stress and the risk of falling behind on bills.

- **Building your emergency fund:** With more income, you can save money for unexpected events like car repairs, medical emergencies, or job loss. As discussed in the previous chapter, this financial buffer provides a safety net and prevents financial instability caused by temporary setbacks.

- **Debt management:** Higher income makes it easier to manage debt repayments and to stay out of bad debt. You can avoid high-interest loans and credit card debt, which can significantly strain your finances.

- **Savings and investments:** More income allows you to save and invest for the future. This can include retirement savings, a down payment on a house, or your children's education. Growing your wealth through savings and investments increases your financial security in the long run while allowing you to enjoy your life today.

Unfortunately, as the income for people increases, their taste also increases, often resulting in even more debt than when they made less. I was recently speaking to one of my daughter's medical providers. She shared with me some of her monthly expenses, which include rent for over five thousand dollars, paying three to four thousand dollars to whittle down her almost half a million dollars in student loan debt, and the large overhead for her private practice.

She went on to say that many people think doctors make a lot, but after paying expenses, she doesn't have any savings left and, therefore, cannot afford a home. As I listened to her, I had so many ideas on how she could manage some of the expenses she mentioned, but this was just a moment to listen. Each time I have these conversations, it is a sobering reality of why everyone should learn even the basics of money management.

How to Assess Your Current Income and Identify Areas for Improvement

Since you've got budgeting under control, let's focus on assessing your current income and finding areas for improvement. **Here's a two-pronged approach:**

1. **Analyze Potential Income Streams:**

    - **Break down your income:** You have already done this in the budgeting section.

    - **Evaluate your earning potential:** Within your current job, are there opportunities for raises, promotions, or increased commissions? Could you take on additional responsibilities or negotiate a higher salary?

    - Never settle for the thought that there are no opportunities for promotions, either inside or outside of your company. I discussed in an earlier chapter how I helped a client land a job within her company that she did not think she was qualified for, at an almost 40% salary increase.

    - **Explore additional income streams:** Do you have skills or hobbies that could be monetized through freelancing, online businesses, or selling crafts?

2. **Benchmark and Research:**

    - **Industry standards:** Research average salaries for your job title, location, and experience level. This will help you understand your current position relative to the market.

    - **Upskilling and certifications:** Are there specific skills or certifications that could increase your earning potential in your current field?

- **Job market:** Is your current industry growing or shrinking? Are there in-demand skills you could develop to position yourself for higher-paying opportunities in the future?

By combining this income analysis with everything you have learned about budgeting, you can identify areas for improvement:

- **Maximize current income:** If research shows you're underpaid, consider negotiating a raise or exploring opportunities for increased compensation within your current role or finding a job in another organization.

- **Develop additional income streams:** If your current income allows room for growth, explore side hustles that leverage your existing skills or interests (more on this in the next section).

- **Invest in yourself:** Consider taking courses or certifications that can enhance your skill set and open doors to higher-paying opportunities.

Following these steps will provide you with valuable insights into your current income situation. This will allow you to identify areas where you can potentially increase your earnings and improve your overall financial situation.

Expanding Your Income Horizons: Side Hustles, Investments, and Passive Income

If you want to achieve short-term or long-term goals, you must find ways to increase your income. For most individuals, a job or a single income stream will not make it happen. **Here's a breakdown of three popular strategies for increasing your income:**

1. **Side Hustles: Earn Extra with Active Effort**

Side hustles involve actively working extra hours to generate income. They offer flexibility but require commitment.

Here are some ideas to consider:

- **Freelancing:** Leverage your existing skills in writing, editing, graphic design, or programming on platforms like Upwork or Fiverr.

- **Online Tutoring:** Share your knowledge! If you have subject matter expertise, you can tutor students in person or online through different platforms.

- **The Sharing Economy:** Drive for Uber, Lyft, or Doordash, or offer delivery services to earn money on your own schedule.

- **Content Creation:** Monetize your passions! Build a following on a blog, YouTube channel, or social media platform and explore advertising, sponsorships, or affiliate marketing.

- **Odd Jobs and Services:** Offer handyman services, pet sitting, house cleaning, or errands running through local apps or by connecting with people in your community.

2. **Investments: Grow Your Wealth Over Time**

Investments involve putting your money to work for you, which will generate returns during your investing period. They offer long-term benefits but come with inherent risks. **Here are some options to explore:**

- **Stocks and Funds:** Invest in the stock market by buying shares of companies or diversify your investment exposure by investing in funds such as Mutual Funds, Index Funds, or Exchange-Traded Funds (ETFs). This can offer good returns, but remember, the stock market fluctuates, so I would not recommend investing for the short term.

- **Peer-to-Peer Lending:** Loan money to individuals or businesses through online platforms and earn interest on the repayments. To reduce your risk, use a platform that has a track record because it is important to assess borrower's risk before investing.

3. **Passive Income Streams: Earn While You Sleep (Almost!)**

Passive income streams generate income with minimal ongoing effort after the initial setup. They offer long-term benefits but often require upfront work.

Here are some examples:

- **Rental Income:** Rent out a spare room, vacation property, or parking space. While passive, it may require occasional maintenance or addressing tenants' concerns. If you want to be hands-off, you can hire a property management company.

- **Royalties:** Earn royalties from creative works like eBooks, music, or photography through licensing or sales platforms. Building an audience or portfolio might be required initially.

- **Affiliate Marketing:** Promote other companies' products on your website or social media and earn commissions for each sale. This requires audience building and marketing efforts upfront.

Choosing the Right Path: Evaluating Income Opportunities

Not all side hustles or investments are good for you. Before diving in, **consider these factors:**

- **Time Commitment:** How many hours per week can you realistically dedicate?

- **Startup Costs:** Does this venture require any upfront investment (e.g., equipment, inventory)?

- **Skills and Experience:** Do you have the necessary skills, or can you learn them readily?

- **Income Potential:** How much can you realistically earn, and how quickly?

- **Scalability:** Can you grow this income stream over time?

- **Risk Tolerance:** How comfortable are you with the potential risks involved (e.g., market fluctuations in case of investments)?

Bonus Tip: Consider your interests! Choosing an income-producing opportunity that you enjoy can make it more sustainable and potentially lead to greater success.

Tips for balancing multiple income streams with your primary job or responsibilities

Juggling multiple income streams with your main job or responsibilities requires effective time management and organization. You would need to distribute your effort and resources across all streams while upholding your commitment to each. You can very easily become overwhelmed amidst everything going on in your everyday life. **Here are some tips to help you find balance:**

- **Planning and Prioritization:**

  - **Schedule Time Blocking:** Dedicate specific blocks of time in your calendar for each income stream and your primary job. This ensures focused work on each activity and avoids overwhelming multitasking.

  - **Prioritize Ruthlessly:** Identify the most important tasks and focus on completing high-impact activities first.

  - **Utilize Productivity Techniques:** Explore methods like the Pomodoro Technique, where focused work is broken into 25-minute intervals followed by short breaks. This will help to maintain focus and avoid burnout.

- **Streamlining and Delegation:**

  - **Automate Repetitive Tasks:** Look for opportunities to automate repetitive tasks within your income streams or job (e.g., scheduling emails, social media posting). Freeing up time allows you to focus on higher-value activities.

- o **Outsource When Possible:** Consider outsourcing tasks that someone else can do efficiently, freeing up your time for core income-generating activities or essential responsibilities.
- o **Utilize Tools and Apps:** Explore project management tools, time trackers, or communication apps to streamline workflows and improve collaboration across your income streams.

- **Boundaries and Self-Care:**

  - o **Set Clear Boundaries:** Communicate your availability and working hours for each income stream to avoid work bleeding into personal time.
  - o **Learn to Say No:** Don't overload yourself. Don't be afraid to decline additional work if it disrupts your carefully crafted balance.
  - o **Schedule Self-Care:** Make time for activities that help you de-stress and recharge. This will improve your focus and productivity in the long run.

Additional Tips:

- **Consolidate Tasks:** Look for ways to combine tasks across your income streams. For example, if you're creating content for one platform, consider repurposing it for others.
- **Track Your Time:** Monitor your time spent on each income stream. This helps identify areas for improvement and ensures you're allocating time effectively.

- **Re-evaluate Regularly:** As your income streams evolve or your priorities change, revisit your schedule and approach to maintain a healthy balance.

Strategies for Negotiating Salary or Freelance Rates

I know negotiation comes off as intimidating for most people, but it is critical that you speak up for yourself so that your worth is not underestimated, leaving you overstretched and unfulfilled.

Negotiating your salary or freelance rates is a crucial skill for maximizing your income. Here's a not-so-well-known fact. Employers expect you to negotiate, and they have a salary band within which they are working. Let me show you why it's important and how you can approach it effectively:

Why Negotiation Matters

- **Closing the Pay Gap:** Many people, especially women and people of color, are paid a lower salary. Many studies in the U.S. show that the racial and gender gap continues to persist, especially for blacks and Hispanics. But this is also evident in countries like the U.K. Negotiation helps bridge this gap and ensure you're compensated fairly for your skills and experience.

- **Increased Earning Potential:** A successful negotiation can significantly boost your income, impacting your overall financial well-being and the quality of life that you can offer your family. For example, moving into a neighborhood with a better school district for your children.

- **Confidence and Empowerment:** The ability to negotiate effectively builds confidence and empowers you to advocate for yourself in all aspects of your career.

Preparing for the Negotiation

- **Research Market Rates:** Know your worth! Use salary comparison tools and industry publications to understand the average salary for your position, experience level, and location. This equips you with data to back up your requests.

- **Consider the Value You Bring:** Identify your unique skills and experiences that will benefit the employer or client. Always quantify your accomplishments whenever possible (e.g., increased sales by X% or saved the company Y dollars).

- **Set Realistic Goals:** Don't be unreasonable. Research a realistic target range for your desired salary or freelance rate, considering factors such as your experience and the current market environment for your industry.

- **Practice Your Pitch:** Rehearse your negotiation points beforehand. Anticipate potential objections from the employer or client and prepare counterarguments. Doing your research and highlighting your accomplishments will go a long way in supporting your arguments.

Advocating for Yourself at the Negotiation Table

- **Focus on Value, Not Just Salary:** Highlight the value you bring to the company, not just the "what's in it for me" aspect. Focus on how your skills will benefit their bottom line.

- **Be Prepared to Negotiate:** Don't expect the first offer to be final. Be prepared to counter-offer with data and justification for your desired rate.

- **Negotiate More Than Just Salary:** Many people overlook other amazing benefits they can negotiate upfront, such as paid time off, signing bonuses, or professional development opportunities. I recall one employer with whom I negotiated a work-from-home schedule, which greatly benefited me since I had two young children. It kept me at the company much longer than I would have stayed if I did not have that flexibility.

- **Confidence is Key:** Always project confidence and professionalism in your demeanor and communication.

Negotiating with Clients or Employers

- **Be Clear and Direct:** If the client does not share the salary range with you, have a conversation that clearly communicates your desired salary or freelance rate. This should be commensurate with your experience and the rates that you expect based on your research. Don't leave it open-ended for the employer or client to lowball you. If the client has communicated the salary to you, then the negotiations will begin there. Start above what your bottom line is.

- **Be Willing to Walk Away:** If the negotiation reaches an impasse and the offer doesn't meet your minimum requirements, be prepared to walk away. Remember to consider the overall package, not just the salary.

For example, I remember accepting a position that paid substantially less than I desired. Still, I believed the opportunity was completely aligned with my long-term goals and would round out my experience, culminating in a much higher future income and title. In addition, the health and retirement benefits package and the tuition reimbursement were far superior to my last job. So, while the compensation could have been higher, I felt it was the right move at that point in my career.

Remember: Negotiation is a conversation, not a confrontation. Approach it not only with respect, but also with unwavering confidence in your worth.

From Idea to Opportunity: Generating, Evaluating, and Capitalizing on Business Ideas

Turning your passion into profit starts with a strong business idea. Consider this roadmap to help you generate ideas, **assess their potential, and identify emerging market trends:**

Idea Generation

- **Brainstorming:** Gather your thoughts! List down your interests, hobbies, and skills. What problems do you encounter or see others encounter in their daily lives? What gaps in the market could you address?

- **Look for Inspiration:** Research successful businesses in your area of interest. Attend industry events, read business publications, and explore online resources for inspiration.

- **Talk to People:** Network with potential customers, industry experts, and entrepreneurs. Understand their pain points and unmet needs. This can spark valuable ideas.

Evaluating Your Ideas

- **Market Demand:** Is there a real need for your product or service? Conduct market research to understand the target audience, their needs, and existing solutions.

- **Competition:** Who are your competitors? Analyze their strengths and weaknesses. Can you offer a unique value proposition that stands out?

- **Profit Potential:** Can you create a sustainable business model? Estimate costs, pricing strategies, and potential revenue streams.

Identifying Your Target Market and Feasibility Studies

- **Quantitative Research:** Conduct surveys, polls, or focus groups to gather data on customer needs, preferences, and buying habits. Using social media can be a quick and easy tool.

- **Qualitative Research:** Interview potential customers and industry experts to gain deeper insights into their thoughts and challenges.

- **Feasibility Study:** Create a formal document outlining your business idea, market analysis, competitive landscape, financial projections, and operational plan. This helps assess the viability of your idea.

Identifying Emerging Trends

- **Stay Informed:** Follow industry publications, attend conferences, and network with thought leaders to stay updated on emerging trends and technologies.

- **Analyze Consumer Behavior:** Pay attention to changing consumer habits and preferences. What are people buying more of? What problems are they facing in new areas?

- **Think Outside the Box:** Don't be afraid to combine existing ideas in new ways. Sometimes, the most innovative solutions come from unexpected intersections.

Capitalizing on Opportunities

- **Move Quickly:** In a fast-paced market, capitalize on emerging trends before they become saturated. Once you establish yourself as a voice in that industry, you may begin to stand out as an authority and credibility in your field.

- **Be Adaptable:** Be prepared to pivot your idea or business model as market conditions evolve.

- **Build a Strong Team:** As you begin to grow your business, surround yourself with talented people who complement your skills and share your goal. Create a business procedure that new team members can easily follow.

A successful business idea is an amalgamation of market demand, personal passion, and strategic planning.

Reflection

- How can you increase your income in the short term?
    - Consider taking on freelance work or a part-time job.
    - Explore opportunities for overtime or additional shifts at your current job.
- How can you increase your income in the long term?
    - Invest in further education or training to enhance your skills and qualifications.
    - Explore career advancement opportunities within your current field or industry.
- Are there any entrepreneurial opportunities you've been considering?
    - Reflect on your interests, skills, and market trends to identify potential business ideas.

- Research the feasibility and market demand for your potential entrepreneurial ventures.

Key Takeaways

- Income and entrepreneurship are vital for wealth accumulation and a better life. They play different but complementary roles in financial success.

- A steady income from a job provides stability, allowing for comfortable living, saving for the future, and enjoying some luxuries.

- Entrepreneurship offers the potential for higher income and innovation but comes with risk and fluctuating earnings.

- Both approaches can lead to financial security and a better quality of life, depending on personal goals and risk tolerance.

- Financial stability is strongly correlated with income, allowing for meeting basic needs, building emergency funds, managing debt, and saving/investing for the future.

- Assessing your income involves analyzing current income sources, evaluating earning potential, and exploring additional income streams or opportunities for growth.

- Balancing multiple income streams requires effective time management, prioritization, and self-care to avoid burnout.

- Strategies for increasing income include side hustles, investments, and passive income streams, each with its own benefits and considerations.

Increased Income and Entrepreneurship

- Negotiating salary or freelance rates is essential for maximizing income potential and should be approached with confidence and preparation.

- Generating and evaluating business ideas requires creativity, market research, and feasibility studies to identify profitable opportunities and capitalize on emerging trends.

Now that we have covered the various ways to increase your income, the next chapter ventures into the depths of investing for the future. We'll discuss how to put your hard-earned money to work for you, building wealth for the long term and securing your financial future. From exploring different investment options to navigating risk and building a strong portfolio, this chapter equips you with the knowledge to make informed investment decisions and watch your money grow.

Chapter Eight

Investing For the Future

"In the long run, it's not just how much money you make that will determine your future prosperity. It's how much of that money you put to work by saving it and investing it."
—Peter Lynch

Investing is crucial for long-term financial growth and security. It allows you to grow your money faster than saving alone, potentially outpacing inflation and building wealth over time. This prepares you for future goals like retirement or unexpected expenses, providing peace of mind, and financial stability. We have introduced investment in later chapters, but now, we will go in-depth to solidify your confidence, empower you to take action, and start building your financial future through investing.

ABCs of Investment: Risk, Return, Diversification, and Asset Allocation

Investing is a powerful tool for growing your wealth over time, but it's not without its intricacies. Understanding these concepts is essential before diving in. I will provide simplified examples throughout each section to help you better conceptualize the terms.

- **Risk and Return:**

  - **Risk:** This refers to the chance of losing part or (in some cases) all of your investment. Generally, investments with a higher potential return have a higher risk. For example, stocks can offer significant growth but fluctuate more than bonds.

  - **Return:** This is the profit you earn on your investment. It can come in different forms. Most commonly, interest, capital appreciation (increase in the value of the investment), or dividends (a portion of a company's income paid out to anyone who owns their stock).

    - **Gains & Losses:** A gain occurs when the price of an investment rises above the price you paid for it, and a loss occurs when the price falls below what you invested. If you sell the investment, you will have a realized gain/loss at the time of sale. If you hold on to the investment and look at the value in a future period, you will have an unrealized gain/loss, depending on whether the price increases or decreases.

    - Here is a simplified real-life example to explain the terms. Last January, you invested $50 in a company's share (stock). This year, the stock price increased to $60. At the end of the year, the company was profitable and decided to distribute some of its income to the shareholders. Each shareholder gets $1 for each stock they own.

- Since you own one share, at the end of the year, your return in the form of an unrealized gain on the stock is $10, plus the $1 dividends for a total of $11. If the price had fallen to $40, and you sold the stock after receiving the dividends, you would have a net unrealized loss of $9, which is the $10 loss from the decline in price plus the $1 dividends that you received.
  - **Risk Tolerance:** This is the amount of risk that you are willing to take when you invest. It is a very important step in deciding what to invest in. For example, you may decide to never invest in an individual stock, but you would be willing to invest in an S&P 500 mutual fund since it spreads the risk across 500 different companies.

- **Diversification:**
  - As we have established back in Chapter 3, diversification is the cornerstone of a sound investment strategy. It involves spreading your investments across different asset classes to minimize risk.
  - **Asset Classes:** These are broad categories of investments, each with its own risk-return profile. **Some common examples include:**
    - **Stocks:** You own shares in a company, offering the potential for capital appreciation and dividends. Anyone can own shares in any company traded on the New York Stock Exchange. The terms share and

stock are used interchangeably. There are thousands of stocks. Some examples include Apple, Amazon, Nike, and Google.

- **Bonds:** Debt issued by governments, municipalities, or companies, providing a steady stream of income in the form of interest payments. Bonds are usually issued to raise money. Let's say New York City needs to construct a new bridge costing $100 million. They issue a 10-year bond. Anyone who purchases the bond (bondholder) becomes a creditor of New York City and will receive interest on the bond twice per year for ten years. The bond will mature/expire in 10 years, and bondholders will receive their investment back.

- **Real Estate:** Owning property that can generate rental income and appreciate in value over time. A simple example is owning your own home. Over the past several years, home ownership has become controversial. I only find that to be true if you have purchased a home that is way above your means. Depending on the setup of your home and the jurisdiction you live in, you can earn extra income by renting it out as an Airbnb, for TV show production, and so much more.

- **Funds:** There are several different types of funds that you can invest in for further diversification. The most common are mutual funds, index funds, and exchange-traded funds. Essentially, the general idea of all funds is the same, but there are some differences between each fund. A large pool of stocks is placed in one fund so that your investment risks are reduced. For example, you may have a fund like the S&P 500 Mutual Fund that has 500 different stocks.

- **Cash Equivalents:** Low-risk investments like high-yield savings accounts or money market funds, offering easy access to your money but lower returns. These are great accounts for your emergency fund.

- **Asset Allocation:**

    o This refers to the strategy of dividing your investment portfolio among different asset classes based on your risk tolerance, investment goals (e.g., saving for college or retirement), and time horizon (how long you want to invest for).

    o Younger investors with a longer time horizon can typically tolerate more risks and allocate a higher percentage to stocks for growth potential. As you approach retirement, you might shift your allocation towards bonds and cash equivalents for income and stability.

    o With that said, even younger investors may shy away from individual stocks. In that same vein, investors nearing retirement may decide that a certain portion of their investment still belongs in stocks, despite the riskiness of stocks. It is, therefore, very important to assess your risk tolerance before you begin investing. You can do it independently or work with a financial coach or advisor to accomplish this.

Getting a good grasp of these concepts will put you steps ahead on your journey and also help you avoid pitfalls.

Aligning Your Investments with Your Goals: Prioritizing for the Future

Think about your **Action Plan**. Can you see how important it is and how it relates to investing and wealth creation? I can't emphasize this enough: everything about your investing should be consistent with that plan.

Since you already have a **SMART** principle-based action plan, let's focus on identifying and prioritizing your investment goals based on their time horizon.

Step 1: Brainstorm Your Goals

- We defined investment goals in Chapter 3. Go back to this chapter and do the exercise if you haven't defined your investment goals yet.

Step 2: Prioritize Your Goals

Back in Chapter 3, we discussed the importance of aligning your action plan with your investment goals. **You can refer back to that section for a more wholesome perspective than the brief points below:**

- **Essential vs. Aspirational:** Distinguish between needs (emergency fund) and wants (luxury car).

- **Time Sensitivity (Short, Mid, And Long-Term Goals):** Goals with stricter timelines (down payment in a year) should be prioritized over those with more flexibility (retirement in 20 years).

- **Personal Values:** Consider your priorities. If you value travel, a vacation fund may be more vital than a fancy car. We must constantly be realistic about what we can afford without incurring excessive debt.

Step 3: Match Your Goals with Investment Options

- **Short-Term (<1 year):** Consider low-risk, liquid investments such as high-yield savings accounts, certificates of deposit (CDs), and money market accounts. These provide easy access to your assets when needed but have lesser potential returns. During the low-interest rate environment, I never recommended CDs, but when interest rates climb, they are an option to explore. But be conscious of their limitations. That means you must pay a penalty if you withdraw your money before it matures.

- **Mid-Term (1-5 years):** Consider a mix of moderate-risk investments. Balanced mutual funds or index funds can offer some growth potential while maintaining some stability. You could also allocate a portion of the money to bonds for income and stability.

- **Long-Term (> 5 years):** Focus on higher-growth potential investments like stocks or stock mutual funds. These investments will experience fluctuations but have the potential for significant returns over the long haul. Real estate investments are also a valuable option, as they not only provide potential income but also asset appreciation. All investments should be made based on your risk tolerance.

Step 4: Review and Revise Regularly

- Your goals and circumstances might change over time. Review your investment plan at a minimum annually to ensure your asset allocation aligns with your evolving priorities.

- As you achieve short-term goals, seek opportunities to move funds towards mid or long-term goals.

If you follow these procedures consistently, you will see your wealth grow over time through investments that fit your risk-return profile.

Why Aligning Risk, Time Horizon, and Investment Goals is Crucial

Imagine sprinting a marathon – it wouldn't end well, right? The same applies to investing without considering your risk tolerance and time horizon. Here's why aligning these three factors is essential:

Matching Risk with Goals:

- **Risk and Reward are Partners:** Higher returns on your investment often come with a higher risk. If your goal is a short-term emergency fund, investing in volatile stocks wouldn't be wise. You need quick access to the money; market fluctuations could jeopardize that.

- **Preserving vs. Growing:** For short-term goals or those crucial for financial security (emergency fund, down payment), prioritize lower-risk investments that focus on protecting your capital over high growth. For long-term goals like retirement, you have time to ride out market fluctuations and potentially benefit from higher-risk, growth-oriented investments like stocks.

Time Horizon Defines the Direction Investment:

- **Short-Term Needs:** Need the money soon? Invest in highly liquid assets (easily converted to cash) like savings accounts or short-term bonds.

- **Long-Term Growth:** Is your retirement decades away? You may be able to tolerate more risk. This opens up the opportunity to invest in stocks or funds that have the potential for significant growth over extended periods, allowing time to weather short-term market dips.

Alignment Ensures Success:

- Investing with the wrong strategy can be difficult. Knowing your risk tolerance and matching it to your goals through appropriate investments will allow you to sleep easier at night. Set yourself up for success by aligning your investments with your objectives and time frame. Your emergency fund will be there when needed, your child's college education will be appropriately paid, and you will be on track for a fulfilling retirement.

Investment Options: Building Your Financial Toolbox

Now that you understand the importance of aligning goals with risk tolerance and time horizon, **let's explore some popular investment options:**

1. **Stocks: Ownership Shares in Companies**

    - **Investing in a Piece of the Pie:** Stocks represent ownership shares in a company. When a company performs well, its stock price typically increases. As described earlier in the chapter, you can profit from owning a stock through price appreciation, also known as capital gains. Certain companies also offer dividends, which are regular cash payments distributed quarterly to their shareholders who own the stock as of a certain date.

    - **High Growth Potential, Higher Risk:** Stocks can offer significant long-term returns, but they also come with risks. Stock prices fluctuate significantly due to market conditions, company performance, and overall economic factors.

2. **Bonds: IOUs from Borrowers**

    - **Lending Your Money, Earning Interest:** Bonds are essentially IOUs issued by governments, municipalities, or corporations. When you purchase a bond, you're essentially loaning money to the issuer. In return, you receive regular interest payments and the return of your principal amount when the bond matures.

    - **Lower Risk, Lower Return:** Bonds are generally considered less risky than stocks because they offer a fixed income stream and return of your principal. However, they typically offer lower potential returns compared to stocks.

3. **Mutual Funds: Bundled Investments for Diversification**

    - **Professional Management & Diversification:** Mutual funds pool money from multiple investors and invest it in a basket of assets like stocks, bonds, or a combination of both. This provides instant diversification, reducing risk compared to owning individual stocks. Professional fund managers handle the investment selection and management. Most mutual funds charge different types of fees.

    - **Variety & Choice:** With over 7,000 Mutual funds in the United States, you can invest in funds based on specific sectors, asset classes, or investment goals. This allows you to choose a fund that aligns with your risk tolerance and investment objectives. Fees and expenses vary across each fund.

4. **Real Estate: Investing in Property**

    - **Tangible Assets & Long-Term Potential:** Real estate involves owning and managing properties like houses, apartments, or commercial buildings. You can generate income through rent payments and potentially benefit from property value appreciation over time.

- **Higher Investment & Management Needs:** Real estate requires a significant upfront investment and ongoing management responsibilities such as maintenance, repairs, and addressing the tenants' concerns. When compared to other forms of investment, selling your real estate is a much longer process. You can choose to invest in real estate by purchasing real estate investment trusts (REITs). Similar to stocks, publicly traded REITs can be bought and sold daily.

How do you choose which option fits your needs? **This is where investment strategies come in:**

Investment Strategies

These broad approaches guide your investment decisions based on your goals and risk tolerance. **Let's look at three common strategies:**

- **Growth Investing:** This strategy focuses on companies with high growth potential, even if their stock prices seem high currently. Growth investors believe future earnings will justify the higher price tag. This strategy is suitable for investors with a long time horizon and a higher risk tolerance since younger, high-growth companies can be volatile. An example of a growth company is Tesla.

- **Value Investing:** This approach focuses on undervalued stocks, meaning stocks that appear to be trading for less than the company's real worth, also known as the intrinsic value. These are generally stocks in more mature companies, such as Walmart. Value investors believe the market has overlooked these stocks, and their prices will eventually rise to reflect their true worth. Value investing requires patience and a longer time horizon, but it can offer significant returns if successful.

- **Income Investing:** This strategy prioritizes investments that generate regular income, such as dividend-paying stocks, bonds, or REITs. Income investors aim for a steady stream of income to supplement their lifestyle or retirement needs. This approach is suitable for investors seeking to increase their current income but can be used at any stage in your investment journey.

Choosing the Right Mix

There's no one-size-fits-all solution. Many investors use a combination of strategies to create a diversified portfolio that aligns with their overall financial goals. For example, a young investor with a long time horizon might allocate a portion of their portfolio to growth stocks for long-term growth, while also holding income-generating investments like bonds for stability and current income.

Here is a scenario to help:

Million Dollar Decisions: Tailoring Investments to Reach Goals

Reaching the "**millions**" mark is an ambitious yet achievable goal with the right investment strategy. Let's explore how two individuals, Sarah (a young salaried professional) and Michael (an established entrepreneur) can tailor their investment mix to maximize their potential wealth:

Sarah, the Young Professional (25 years old):

- **Salary Earner:** Sarah earns a steady income but has limited capital for upfront investments.

- **Long-Time Horizon:** Sarah has 35+ years until retirement, allowing her to take on higher risk for potential long-term growth.

- **Moderate Risk Tolerance:** Sarah is comfortable with some risks but wants to avoid excessive volatility.

Investment Strategy:

- **Growth Investing (70%):** A significant portion (70%) of Sarah's portfolio can be allocated to growth-oriented investments. **This could include:**

    - **Index Funds:** Investing in broad market index funds that track a specific market segment provides instant diversification and exposure to high-growth potential companies.

    - **Growth Stock ETFs:** ETFs focused on specific sectors with high-growth potential - like consumer goods or healthcare - that can offer concentrated exposure to these industries.

    - Individual Stocks across the technology and renewable energy sectors.

- **Value Investing (20%):** Allocating 20% to value investing allows Sarah to potentially benefit from undervalued stocks that could appreciate significantly in the future. She may choose to purchase stocks or funds that own stocks such as Walmart and Target.

- **Income Investing (10%):** A small portion can be invested in income-generating assets like dividend-paying stocks or REITs. She can choose to use that income to supplement her current income or reinvest it in her portfolio.

Michael, the Established Entrepreneur (55 years old):

- **Entrepreneur:** Michael has accumulated significant capital from his successful business ventures.

- **Shorter Time Horizon:** With retirement approaching in 10 years, Michael needs to focus on capital preservation while still generating some growth.

- **Lower Risk Tolerance:** As Michael nears retirement, he prioritizes minimizing risk and protecting his accumulated wealth.

Investment Strategy:

- **Income Investing (40%):** A larger portion of Michael's portfolio is allocated to income-generating assets. **This could include:**
    - **Dividend-paying Stocks:** Companies with a history of consistent dividend payments provide a reliable stream of income for Michael during his retirement.

- o **REITs:** Investing in Real Estate Investment Trusts allows Michael to benefit from rental income and potential property value appreciation without the hassle of direct property management. He receives income through dividends paid out quarterly or monthly.

- o **Bonds:** Investing in different types of bonds to lock in income regardless of what cycle the market is in when he retires.

- **Value Investing (30%):** Allocating 30% to value investing offers Michael the chance for additional growth while focusing on undervalued companies with lower risk.

- **Growth Investing (30%):** Michael feels confident that even if there is a market downturn, his income from investing plus the rental income that he currently receives will cover him. He, therefore, continues to invest a third of his portfolio in growth companies.

Keep in mind:

- **Reaching millions takes time and discipline:** There is no one path to becoming a millionaire, but it is possible if you are consistent and create different strategies.

- I began investing at 22 in my retirement plan. I was only putting the amount that my company matched. Once I started my career, I steadily increased how much I put away until I maxed out the annual contribution. Another key thing that I did was to learn how to manage my retirement on my own to reduce fees. I created an investment strategy and remained consistent. I periodically rebalanced my portfolio and was able to build my retirement to over one million dollars before 48. So YES, you can do this too! I had no magical skills. I just took the time to learn just like you are doing now.

- **Seek Professional Guidance:** Consulting a financial coach can be invaluable, especially for complex situations or significant investment decisions.

Keeping Your Portfolio on Track: Monitoring, Adjusting, and Staying Up-to-date

The journey to achieving your financial goals isn't a set-it-and-forget-it process. Just like a well-maintained car, your investment portfolio needs regular monitoring and adjustments to ensure it continues to drive you toward success.

Importance of Monitoring

- **Early Detection of Issues:** Regularly monitoring your investments allows you to identify potential problems early on. A sudden drop in a stock price or a decline in a fund's performance can be a red flag that needs investigation. While it does not mean you should sell this investment, you should review it to understand why it fluctuated, in order to decide what your next step will be.

- **Performance Evaluation:** Tracking your portfolio's performance helps you assess whether it's on track to meet your goals. Are you achieving the desired returns? Is your asset allocation still aligned with your risk tolerance?

- **Timely Adjustments:** Monitoring allows you to make adjustments before they become crucial. If your risk tolerance has changed or market conditions have shifted, you can rebalance your portfolio to stay on course.

Evaluating and Adjusting Your Portfolio

- **Frequency:** The frequency of monitoring depends on your investment style and risk tolerance. Aggressive investors might check daily, while conservative investors might review quarterly or semi-annually. Set a schedule that works for you. I don't recommend daily or even weekly, unless you are trading.

- **Performance Analysis:** Compare how your investment is performing to the goals that you set. If your return is not what you expected, first do some investigation. Then decide what adjustment you should make.

- **Asset Allocation Review:** If the amount of risk that you are willing to take (your risk tolerance) has changed, or there has been changes in the stock market or a particular stock, then you may decide that you need to rebalance your portfolio (i.e. shift your investment choices). For example, at one point, 2 stocks made up almost 50% of my portfolio. I strategically sold shares of both during 2020, and purchased other stocks to reduce the risk I had in those two stocks and to add more diversification to my portfolio.

- **Tax Implications:** Consider tax implications when adjusting. Selling investments from a taxable account might trigger capital gains taxes. Speak to your tax advisor.

Staying Up-to-date

- **Market News:** Stay updated on economic news, major market events, and things going on with the company that could impact your investments. Financial news websites, reputable investment publications, and annual reports of companies you invest in can be valuable sources of information. A word of caution, however, be careful of what you consume on the news because if you listen to 5 different analysts, you may get 5 different opinions. The best way to position yourself is to take the time to educate yourself so that you can filter out the noise.

- **Investment Research:** Conduct ongoing research on your existing and prospective investments. Review analyst reports, industry trends, and company fundamentals to make informed decisions.

- **Professional Guidance:** Consulting a financial coach or advisor can be especially helpful, particularly for complex portfolios or when navigating major life changes. They can offer personalized advice based on your specific circumstances and goals.

Important Note:

- **Don't Panic Sell:** Market fluctuations are inevitable. Focus on your long-term goals and avoid emotional reactions to short-term dips.

- **Don't Buy on Tips:** Many people jump on the bandwagon and purchase investments from tips by social media influencers or news headlines. I did that early on in my investing career and lost over $10,000. I knew better because I was the president of my stock market investment club, but I was being greedy. Take my experience as a cautionary tale. Do your own research.

- **Discipline is Key:** Monitoring and managing your investments takes discipline. Set aside time for regular reviews and stick to your investment plan.

- **Review Your Goals:** As your life evolves, your financial goals might change. Review your investment strategy periodically to ensure it remains aligned with your evolving needs.

Reflection

- How does your investment choices align with your long-term financial goals?

    o Consider your specific investments and how they contribute to your overall financial objectives. Are they helping you progress toward your goals, or do they need adjustments?

- Are there any adjustments you need to make to your investment strategy?

    o Reflect on whether your current strategy is effective, considering your financial goals. Are there areas where you could improve or reallocate investments to better align with your objectives?

Key Takeaways

- **Investing Fundamentals:** Investing is crucial for long-term financial growth and security. It allows you to grow your money faster than saving alone and prepares you for future goals like retirement or unexpected expenses.

- **ABCs of Investment:** Understanding Risk, Return, Diversification, and Asset Allocation is essential before investing:

    - **Risk and Return:** Higher potential returns come with higher risks. Stocks offer growth but fluctuate more, while bonds provide steady income but lower returns.

    - **Diversification:** Spread investments across different asset classes to minimize risk.

    - **Asset Allocation:** Divide your portfolio based on risk tolerance, goals, and time horizon.

- **Aligning Investments with Goals:** Prioritize essential goals, considering time sensitivity and personal values. Match goals with appropriate investment options.

- **Investment Strategies:** Choose from growth, value, or income investing based on your goals and risk tolerance, or use a combination for a diversified portfolio.

- **Monitoring and Adjusting:** Regularly monitor your investments for early detection of issues, evaluate performance, and adjust asset allocation as needed. Stay up-to-date with market news and research.

- **Seeking Professional Guidance:** Consulting a financial coach or advisor can provide valuable insights, especially for complex situations or significant investment decisions.

- **Discipline and Long-Term Focus:** Consistent investing over time, coupled with smart strategies, increases your chances of achieving your financial goals. Avoid emotional reactions to market fluctuations and stick to your investment plan.

Hold on to that picture of a future free from financial worries, to that dream of no longer being chained to a desk job, if you crave something different. The freedom to travel the world or pursue long-held passions; this chapter brings you a step further to that dream, but there's more to cover: Financial independence – that exhilarating state of self-sufficiency – which might seem like a distant dream. Still, with the right techniques and a commitment to long-term planning, it's closer than you think. Yes, you can go from zero to millions. Join me in the next chapter as we explore the path to financial freedom – equipping you with the knowledge and tools to unlock your full financial potential.

Part Three

Sustaining Financial Growth and Stability

"Financial growth and stability are not just about the numbers; they are the fruits of consistent planning, disciplined action, and a mindset focused on long-term prosperity and leaving a legacy."

Chapter Nine

Securing Financial Independence

"Growing wealth is never about how much you make. It is always about how you use what you make."
—**Tanya Taylor**

Imagine Luis, a talented graphic designer. For years, Luis has dreamt of quitting his stressful agency job and traveling the world, soaking up inspiration for his art. But the bills pile up, and financial security feels out of reach. This chapter is for Luis and for anyone who desires freedom from financial worries. Here, we'll break down the concept of Financial Independence, showing you how to build a roadmap to a life where you answer to your dreams, not a paycheck. Through clear steps and relatable examples, you'll gain the knowledge and tools to transform your financial reality and unlock the door to a future filled with freedom and possibility.

Why Financial Independence Matters: Owning Your Future

Financial independence isn't just about having a fancy car or a big house. It's about having control over your time and choices. **Consider this:**

- **No More Alarm Clock:** You wake up when you want because you're not tied to a job you might not even enjoy. You can pursue your passions, whether it's painting, writing, or traveling the world.

- **Calmness and Confidence:** Financial worries can be a huge burden. Financial independence gives you a safety net that lets you breathe easier, knowing you can face unexpected expenses or even take a break from work without financial stress.

- **Freedom to Choose:** You get to decide how you spend your days. Volunteer for a cause you care about, spend more time with family or finally start that business idea you've always had. The choice is yours!

Financial independence isn't about getting rich quickly. It's about smart planning and responsible saving to build a secure future. Remember that mountain at the start of chapter three? It takes time and effort to pull each of the steps to get you up, but the view from the top is amazing! The good news is that anyone can achieve financial independence with the right knowledge and dedication.

This chapter will be your guide, showing you the steps to take control of your finances and unlock the door to freedom. To realize the benefits above, you must evaluate your current financial condition.

Assessing Your Current Financial Situation

You can better understand your current financial situation if you have already started keeping track of and analyzing your income and expenses (from Chapter 5), in which case you just want to grab your budget/spending plan. To make the most of what you have and go deeper, we will summarize what you need below. This will give you a second chance to stop stalling and get this done. **Do the following:**

- **Gather Your Financial Documents:**
  - Bank statements (checking & savings)
  - Credit card statements.
  - Loan statements (mortgage, car, etc.)
  - Investment account statements (if applicable)
  - Paystubs or income summaries

- **Categorize Your Income:**
  - List all your income sources: salary, bonuses, side hustles, rental income, etc.

- **Categorize Your Expenses:**
  - Using your spending data, categorize your expenses into groups like housing, food, transportation, utilities, debt payments, entertainment, etc.

- **Calculate Your Net Worth:**
  - This is the difference between your assets and liabilities. Assets are things you own with value, such as cash, house, or investments. Liabilities are what you owe, such as credit card debt, mortgage payments, etc.
  - Net Worth = Assets - Liabilities

- **Analyze Your Cash Flow:**
    - Look at your income and expenses over a specific period (month, quarter, year). Are you spending more than you earn? If so, by how much?

- **Identify Areas for Improvement:**
    - Using your spending data, pinpoint areas where you can potentially cut back or optimize spending.

- **Review Your Financial Goals:**
    - Do your current spending habits align with your short-term and long-term financial goals (e.g., saving for a down payment, building an emergency fund, retiring early)?

- **Celebrate Achievements:**
    - Recognize the progress you've already made in tracking your spending and analyzing your habits.

You should keep track of your progress toward your goals and make changes as needed by reviewing your finances regularly.

A Comprehensive Roadmap For Financial Independence

Now, just like baking a cake where we have a variety of ingredients, you will begin fitting all the different pieces of your wealth roadmap together. Think of your plans as a well-oiled machine working together. In the previous chapter and with great depth, **we have gone through each of these:**

- **Budget/Spending Plan:** This is the foundation. As we have seen, it allocates your income towards various expenses, including debt payments, savings goals, and potential investments.

- **Credit:** Maintain good credit, in case you want to leverage other people's money for investment such as real estate.

- **Debt Management Plan:** This tackles your debt strategically, freeing up cash flow in the long run.

- **Savings Plan (Emergency Fund):** This acts as a safety net for emergencies, preventing you from getting back into debt.

- **Investment Plan:** This allows your money to grow over time, building wealth for your future.

All these foundational pieces will give you the information you need to determine how much you will be contributing to your investment plans, whether it is your retirement plan, savings for college, or something else.

Plans that can go hand in hand (simultaneously):

- **Budget/Spending Plan, Credit & Debt Management Plan:** These work together seamlessly. Your budget allocates funds for debt payments outlined in your debt management plan. As you pay down debt, you free up more money in your budget to allocate towards other goals. Your credit is king in reducing your interest rates.

- **Emergency Fund & Investment Plan:** A fully funded emergency fund is crucial before aggressively investing.

Once your emergency fund is established, you can focus on long-term goals through your investment plan.

Plans with some interdependence:

- **Budget/Spending Plan & Savings/Investment Plans:** While you can build these plans simultaneously, your budget should reflect the amount you can realistically allocate towards savings and investments. As your income increases or debt payments decrease, you can adjust your budget to increase savings/investment contributions.

- **Debt Management Plan & Investment Plan:** Ideally, you'd want to minimize high-interest debt before heavily investing. While you can choose the snowball or avalanche method discussed in Chapter 2, when you focus on paying off high-interest debt while making minimum payments on lower-interest debt, you will pay less interest overall. This provides more cash flow to contribute to your investment account with higher growth potential. You should still consider investing even if you have debt, especially if you have employer-sponsored retirement plans with matching contributions.

Steps to Achieve Financial Independence

Here are the steps for attaining financial independence. If you've been using your workbook or journal so far and not just reading to learn, you should have already done most of these.

- Assess Your Current Financial Situation
- Define Your Financial Goals

- **Develop Strategies:**
  - Create a Budget/Spending Plan
  - Work on repairing your credit
  - Develop a Debt Management Plan
  - Create an Emergency Fund
  - Create an Investment Plan
  - Explore ways to Increase Income: Some of you may have already done this, while others are still identifying different avenues to accomplish this.
- Take Action and Monitor Progress (this is ongoing)
- Seek Professional Help: Many people fail to progress in meeting their goals because they need accountability and guidance. Go to my website at growyourwealth10x.com and schedule a complimentary session to learn how I can work with you.

How many of these have you completed?

If you haven't done any of these as yet, take the time to get started now. Come back and pick up once you are caught up. This book is really written in a way to push you to take action, and while you can use your own journal, we have also made it convenient for you by providing the workbook. **Here is an example of how you can put it all together:**

Joseph's Journey to Financial Freedom

Joseph, a 22-year-old college graduate, landed his first job as a hospitality manager. Excited about his newfound independence, he enjoyed a carefree lifestyle. However, a nagging worry about his future prompted him to take control of his finances. Inspired by a chapter on financial planning (sound familiar?), Joseph embarked on a journey towards financial freedom.

Step 1: Unveiling the Reality (Current Financial Situation)

Joseph gathered his financial documents - bank statements, his credit card bill, and his paystubs. He categorized his expenses - surprised to see how much he spent on eating out and entertainment. **Here's a breakdown (hypothetical numbers):**

Category	Amount	Notes
Income		
Monthly Income	$5,000	Monthly Salary
Expenses		
Housing	$2,000	Rent
Debt Payments	1,250	Credit Card ($250) + Student Loans ($250) + Car Lease ($450) + Auto Insurance ($300)
Food	850	Groceries ($300) + Dining Out ($550)
Transportation	330	Public transport ($180) + Gas ($150)
Utilities	220	Phone, Cable & Internet
Daily Expenses	530	Daily Starbucks ($150) + Clothing ($250) + Others (Miscellaneous - $130)
Total Expenses	$5,180	

Step 2: Calculating the Standing (Net Worth)

Joseph calculated his net worth. His only asset was $1,000 cash in his checking account (asset). He owed $5,000 on three credit cards and $45,000 in student loans (liabilities). His net worth stood at a negative -$49,000.

Net Worth = $1,000 (Asset) - $50,000 (Liabilities) = -$49,000

Step 3: Cash Flow Conundrum

Joseph reviewed his income and expenses. He was spending $5,180 monthly, exceeding his $5,000 income by $180. This negative cash flow meant he was living beyond his means and using credit cards to supplement his income.

Step 4: Spotlights on Improvement

Joseph analyzed his spending. Eating out and entertainment were clear areas for cutbacks. He decided to limit eating out to twice a month and find free or low-cost entertainment options. He also decided to get rid of his car (which he barely used) and to forgo buying new clothing since he had many unworn clothing in his closet. This freed up over $1,500 in cash monthly.

Step 5: Goal Setting (The Destination)

Joseph envisioned financial freedom - having enough passive income to cover his expenses comfortably. With the help of his financial coach, he set short-term goals – building an emergency fund of at least $6,000 and paying off his credit card debt in six months. His long-term goal was to build his emergency fund to 6 months of expenses, save for retirement & generate rental income by purchasing a property.

Step 6: Taking Flight (Creating a Plan)

Joseph created a budget, allocating more towards his emergency fund and credit card payments. He researched different debt repayment strategies and decided on the avalanche method, focusing first on the debt with the highest interest rate (his credit card).

- **Adding a Retirement Nest Egg:**
    - **Company Plan:** Luckily, Joseph's company offered a 401(k) with a 5% employer match on his salary contribution. He decided to start by contributing 5% to take advantage of the match - $2,500 annually. Because he contributed to the plan before tax, he realized that his net income didn't change as significantly as he thought.
    - **Individual Retirement Account (IRA):** Joseph researched IRAs and chose a Roth IRA for its tax benefits in retirement. He decided to contribute $2,500 annually. He invested in a financial coach, learned about investing, and felt confident that he would be able to manage this account on his own.

So, his total Annual Savings for retirement was $5,000 or $416 monthly.

Step 7: Soaring High (Taking Action and Monitoring Progress)

Working alongside his coach and a group of like-minded individuals he met along the way, he felt very motivated to achieve his goals. He tracked his expenses diligently, celebrating small victories like sticking to his budget and making additional credit card payments. He reviewed his progress monthly, adjusting his plan as needed.

Joseph's Fast-Track to Financial Freedom: A Multi-Seven-Figure Retirement Dream

The Early Hustle (Month 1-6):

Channeling his newfound financial knowledge into action, **he began to tackle his debt:**

- **Debt Avalanche:** Joseph was determined to conquer his credit card debt. He listed his cards by interest rate, starting with the highest at a whopping 24%. Using the avalanche method, he threw every extra dollar he found in his budget at this card, exceeding the minimum payment. By diligently tracking expenses and avoiding unnecessary spending, he focused first on eliminating this high-interest debt. Meanwhile, he made the minimum payments on his other cards with lower interest rates (around 15% and 8%). Once the high-interest card was paid off, Joseph could then focus on tackling the next card on his list, strategically allocating his extra funds toward that debt.

- **Creating An Emergency Fund:** Within 6 months, he had opened a high-yield savings account, saved almost $3,000 in his emergency fund, and was well on his way to saving at least 6 months of expenses.

Investing for the Future (Month 6 and Beyond)

Joseph, now credit card debt-free and with a safety net, was ready to invest long-term and focus on paying off his student loans.

He researched investment options and decided on a diversified portfolio.

- **Company 401(k):** Joseph decided that since he has youth on his side, he would invest 70% of his money in growth funds and the remaining 30% in value funds. He did not feel that, at this stage in his life, he needed income-investing assets in his portfolio.

- **Roth IRA:** He continued contributing $208 monthly to his Roth IRA for tax-advantaged retirement savings. In this account, he invested mainly in individual stocks and ETFs.

Emergency Fund Build-Up: With the debt monkey off his back, Joseph redirected the extra funds toward his emergency fund.

Increase Student Loan Payoff: Joseph set a 5-year goal to pay off his student loan debt, building in a plan to accelerate payment further if he changes job and begins earning a higher salary.

The Power of Consistency

Joseph stuck to his plan religiously. He continued tracking expenses, finding joy in small indulgences while staying within his budget. He reviewed his progress monthly, adjusting his contributions once he received a raise, and used his bonus to pay down some of his student loans.

The Results Speak for Themselves

- After just 2 years, Joseph had fully funded 6 months of emergency funds and made significant headways in reducing his negative net worth. His investment in his retirement plans was steadily growing, and he had managed to remain debt-free.

- **Savings on Autopilot:** Joseph automated his savings and investments, ensuring a consistent flow of money towards his future.

Fast Forward 10 Years

Joseph, now a Manager of operations, continued his financial discipline. His student loan debt was paid off before the 5-year timeframe he set. His salary had more than doubled in the 10 years, allowing him to max out his retirement plan contributions annually. The power of compound interest worked its magic on his investments, significantly growing his nest egg. A few other wonderful events happened in his life. He got married and now has 2 young children.

Because he had remained disciplined in his finances, with the combined income of his wife, they purchased a beautiful 2-family home where they collect rental income from the second unit. They invest most of this income. They have over $170,000 in their retirement account and are able to take their family on vacations debt-free every year.

The Dream Realized

Joseph and his wife are now 32. If they continue along the same trajectory and invest $3,200 in their retirement monthly, by the time they retire at 57, if they receive an average of 8% return annually, they will have over $3 million in their retirement plan. They are currently using the rental income to fund their children's college education and enjoying vacations with them.

While this is not the complete story of any of my clients, I had one individual that I worked with many years ago. He came very close in the first 10 years, as described. I am no longer in touch, but if he kept that same discipline or even eased up a bit but continued to invest and maintain minimum debt, he would never have to worry about college tuition or retirement.

Lessons Learned from Joseph's Journey

Joseph's story is a testament to the power of taking control of your finances. By following the steps I outline in this book, you can achieve your goals well beyond what you envisioned. Joseph started with 5%. I started with 3%. How much will you start with?

Here is my advice to you. Start where you are. You too can achieve financial freedom and secure a comfortable retirement, no matter your starting point. It's not about how much you earn but about your financial habits and commitment to your goals. If you haven't yet started, start today. Exactly where you are. I am happy to guide you through the process. You will be rewarded! Know that **YOU ARE WORTH IT!**

Reflection

- What steps can you take today to assess your current financial situation and start building a roadmap towards financial independence?

- How can you integrate budgeting, debt management, savings, and investment plans to create a comprehensive strategy for achieving financial freedom?

- What will it take to get started and keep you motivated to remain consistent?

Key Takeaways

- Financial independence is about having control over your time and choices, allowing you to pursue your passions and dreams without financial stress.

- Assessing your current financial situation is crucial for understanding where you stand and setting realistic goals.

- Building an emergency fund is essential to handle unexpected expenses and avoid going into debt.

- Creating a comprehensive roadmap for financial independence involves integrating various financial plans like budgeting, debt management, savings, and investment.

- Steps to achieve financial independence include defining goals, developing strategies, creating a budget, increasing income, managing debt, saving, investing, and seeking professional help if needed.

- Joseph's journey to financial freedom exemplifies the power of financial planning, disciplined saving, and smart investing.

Life throws financial curveballs - recessions, inflation, job losses - you name it. But fear not, future financial freedom fighter! The next chapter equips you with the knowledge and strategies to navigate economic challenges with confidence. You have made it this far. Now, fasten your seat belt and get ready to learn how to weather any financial storm that comes your way!

Chapter Ten

Navigating Economic Challenges

> *"Success is not final, failure is not fatal:*
> *It is the courage to continue that counts."*
> **—Winston Churchill**

Bill Gates. Tech titan. The 90s. Remember that feeling? Dot.com companies were the new gold rush, and Microsoft's stock price was on a victory lap, catapulting Gates to billionaire kingpin status. It was a party fueled by "irrational exuberance," as some stuffy financial types called it.

But then, as with all good parties, the music stopped. In a move that surprised exactly no one who'd studied basic economics, the Dot.com bubble busted wide open. Many tech companies went kaput, and the stock market took a nosedive. I lost somewhere between $10,000 and $15,000. Clearly, I was in on the greed frenzy because I definitely knew and saw all the warning signs, even though I did not study economics!

Microsoft wasn't a total disaster, but it felt the aftershocks for sure. This, my friends, is what we call an economic contraction – the not-so-fun part of the boom-and-bust cycle.

No idea what the boom-and-bust cycle is? It refers to a period of economic expansion (boom) followed by a period of economic decline (bust).

I don't know if I would say Gates got lucky. I think he had something solid that stands the test of time even today.

My decisions were dumb. But You Can Be Smart

My experience is a cautionary tale! Economic cycles are like the weather: sunny today, stormy tomorrow. **Here's the thing to remember:**

- **Boom Times Don't Last:** For everyone, from billionaires to your friendly neighborhood barista, economic expansions will taper off. They're like that amazing sale at your favorite store – eventually, the discounts dry up.

- **Downturns Can Bite:** Recessions are like that surprise downpour that soaks you to the bone. They can wreak havoc on your finances and investments, no matter how much you have.

So, What Can You Do?

Here's where Bill Gates - and everyday people who survived this era - likely had: a solid financial safety net. You, too, **can be a financial sturdy if you take this seriously:**

1. Having an emergency fund helps cover unexpected expenses during downturns (I can't stress this enough, but repetition makes things stick).

2. A diversified investment strategy can help weather economic fluctuations.

3. Living within your means during good times and putting away as much as possible allows you to maintain financial stability during tougher times.

These three things are super important. Get them locked in your brain, and you'll thank me later.

Understanding Economic Cycles and their Impact on Personal Finances

The economy isn't on a steady straight path; it goes through ups and downs in a cyclical pattern known as the economic cycle (sometimes also called the business cycle). This cycle is divided into four main phases: expansion, peak, contraction, and trough.

Expansion is the feel-good part of the cycle. During this time, the economy is growing, people are getting jobs, businesses are profiting, and society is generally feeling optimistic. However, some people still struggle for various reasons within and sometimes out of their control. This growth is often measured by Gross Domestic Product (GDP), which is the total value of goods and services produced in a country. Businesses are hiring more workers to keep up with consumer demand, and this can lead to lower unemployment rates and rising wages.

Peak is the tippy-top of the cycle. The economy has reached its highest point of growth and can't sustain that forever. Things start to level off, and there might be warning signs like inflation, which means prices are going up or interest rates are rising.

Contraction is the downturn. The economy starts to shrink, businesses lay off workers, and unemployment rises. People begin exercising caution by spending less. This is often referred to as a recession, which is defined by the National Bureau of Economic Research (NBER) as a period of significant decline in economic activity that lasts more than a few months.

The trough is the bottom of the cycle. The economy has hit its lowest point, and things are pretty bleak. However, this is also where the seeds of recovery are often sown. The government may start injecting cash into the economy through certain economic policies, including lowering interest rates to allow more borrowing. These actions will incentivize businesses to start investing again in anticipation of better times.

The length of each stage will vary, and there's no perfect science for predicting when the economy will shift from one phase to another. However, understanding these cycles can help you make informed decisions about your finances and career.

Recognizing the Economic Cycle and Adjusting Your Finances

What phase of the economic cycle is prevalent where you are right now? Can you tell?

The thought that you have to figure out, especially when it's the first time you are learning that there's such a thing as the "economic cycle", can be overwhelming. But hang on; there are some things to keep an eye out for in our quest to recognize the economic cycle that we are in. It's not as complicated as it might seem.

Let me walk you through some of the key factors economists consider:

Spotting the Signs:

- **Economic Indicators:** Look at key economic indicators like GDP growth, unemployment rate, inflation rate, and interest rates. Generally, a rising GDP and low unemployment indicate expansion, while a declining GDP and rising unemployment suggest contraction.

- **Stock Market Performance:** While not a foolproof indicator, a strong bull market often coincides with economic expansion, while a bear market can signal a potential contraction. In a bull market, investors are optimistic that the stock prices will rise. In a bear market, the belief is that the stock market will fall.

- **Consumer Confidence:** Consumer confidence surveys gauge people's spending habits. Rising confidence points towards expansion, while falling confidence suggests a potential slowdown.

- **News and Expert Opinions:** Stay informed by following economic news and commentaries from reputable sources. Experts may discuss economic trends and predict future cycles.

Adjusting Your Financial Plans:

- **Expansion:** This is a good time to focus on growing your wealth. Consider increasing contributions to retirement accounts and investing in stocks that might benefit from economic growth. However, be mindful of not taking on excessive risk.

- **Peak:** As the economy nears a peak, it's wise to be more cautious. You might want to diversify your investments to include more stable assets like bonds. Consider contributing more to your emergency fund to weather any potential downturns, including getting laid off.

- **Contraction:** During a recession, focus on financial stability. Prioritize essential expenses and cut back on discretionary spending. This might not be the best time to take on new debt. Focus on keeping your job or finding new income sources if necessary.

- **Trough:** While the economy is at its lowest, opportunities might exist. If you have a secure job and emergency savings, consider investing in beaten-down stocks with long-term potential. However, this requires a strong risk tolerance because most people are tempted to sell when stock prices are falling, but as Warren Buffet says, "to be fearful when others are greedy and to be greedy only when others are fearful". I have found some of my best-performing stocks during a trough.

Tactics for Managing Financial Challenges During Economic Downturns

Economic downturns can throw a wrench into even the most well-oiled financial plans. **Here are some common financial challenges you might face during a recession and some tips for tackling them:**

1. **Job Loss and Reduced Income:**
   - **Challenge:** When businesses are cutting back, layoffs become more common, and bonuses get slashed. This can lead to a sudden loss of income, disrupting your entire financial plan.
   - **Tips:**
     - **Emergency Fund:** This is exactly why having a healthy emergency fund is crucial. It can provide a financial cushion while you search for a new job.
     - **Reduce Expenses:** During a downturn, re-evaluate your budget and cut back on unnecessary spending. This might mean delaying non-essential purchases or finding cheaper alternatives.
     - **Boost Income:** Explore ways to generate additional income, such as freelancing, side hustles, or monetizing hobbies.

2. **Market Volatility:**
   - **Challenge:** Stock markets tend to be more volatile during downturns. Investment values can fluctuate significantly, leading to potential losses.

- **Tips:**

  - **Stay Calm:** Don't panic and do what you might regret. What do you think would have happened if holders of Microsoft stock panicked and sold off their investments? Remember, you only lose money if you sell at a loss, and if you are holding solid companies, they will rebound.

  - **Long-Term Focus:** Downturns are temporary. Maintain a long-term perspective on your investments. Rebalancing your portfolio to reflect your risk tolerance can be helpful.

  - **Diversification:** Your diversified portfolio will keep you firm and unwavering. In chapter 8 I discussed strategically selling off 2 stocks in 2020. I used the proceeds to invest in a few solid companies that had significantly decreased in price because of the stock market crash. Within 2 years, all but one of those stocks that I had purchased had doubled in value and continue to rise.

3. **Tight Credit:**

   - **Challenge:** During economic downturns, banks may tighten lending standards, making it harder to access credit cards, loans, or mortgages.

   - **Tips:**

     - **Maintain Good Credit:** Having a good credit score is always important, but especially so during downturns. It can help you qualify for loans with better terms if needed.

- **Manage Existing Debt**: Pump extra focus on paying off existing debts, especially high-interest ones. This will free up your budget and make you less reliant on additional credit.

- **Explore Alternatives:** Consider alternative financing options like credit unions or peer-to-peer lending platforms, but always borrow responsibly and within your means.

Economic downturns are a normal part of the economic cycle. But being prepared and making smart financial decisions can help you weather the storm and emerge stronger.

How to Identify Opportunities for Financial Growth During Economic Expansion

An economic expansion is a great time to focus on growing your wealth. **Here are some ways to identify opportunities for financial growth during this upswing:**

Investing:

- **Sector Analysis:** Research sectors that tend to perform well during economic expansions. These might include technology, consumer discretionary, or financials.

- **Invest in Growth:** Consider allocating a larger portion of your investment portfolio towards growth stocks. These are companies with the potential for high future earnings growth. However, remember they also tend to be more volatile.

Career and Income Growth:

- **Upskilling and Education:** Invest in yourself by acquiring new skills or certifications that can make you more valuable in the job market. This can lead to promotions, raises, or better job opportunities.

- **Negotiate Your Salary:** During expansion, companies are often more willing to invest in their employees. Research industry salary benchmarks and confidently negotiate for a raise or promotion based on your performance and value.

- **Explore Side Hustles:** The extra income from a side hustle can be used to invest, save for a down payment on a house, or simply improve your overall financial well-being.

Entrepreneurship:

- **Identify Market Needs:** Economic expansions often create new market opportunities. Research consumer trends and identify gaps that your business idea can address. Entrepreneurs can find opportunities in any cycle, so be on the lookout.

- **Seek Funding:** Banks and investors might be more open to funding new ventures during economic booms. Create a solid business plan and be prepared to demonstrate the viability of your idea.

Real Estate:

- **Potential for Appreciation:** During expansions, property prices often rise, so buying them during down cycles (a contraction or trough) when the prices and interest rates are low would be a great way to add real estate as a passive stream of income. While not guaranteed, real estate can be an excellent long-term investment.

- Keep in mind that even in a down cycle, certain geographic locations do not see any significant drop in price and may even continue to see rising prices. You will need to understand the trends in the market that you are interested in. Also, remember that real estate comes with ongoing costs and carries its own set of risks.

Staying Disciplined and Avoiding Financial Pitfalls During Times of Economic Growth

If you are struggling during an economic expansion, you will disappear during a recession. I know it's easy to get swept up in the euphoria of an economic boom. Jobs are plentiful, wages might be rising, and the overall feeling is optimistic. However, this is exactly when financial discipline becomes even more crucial. **Here's why staying grounded and avoiding pitfalls is important during economic expansions:**

1. **Unsustainable Spending Habits:**

    - **Temptation to Overspend:** There's pressure to keep up with the rising standard of living during economic expansion. You might be tempted to splurge on expensive purchases, luxurious vacations, or inflate your lifestyle beyond your means.

- **Debt Trap:** Easy access to credit during expansions can be a recipe for disaster. High-interest debt can quickly spiral out of control, especially if you lose your job during a future downturn.

2. **Ignoring Long-Term Goals:**

    - **Losing Sight of the Future:** Focusing solely on the present boom can make you neglect your long-term financial goals, like retirement planning. You might delay retirement savings or prioritize short-term gratification over long-term wealth building.

    - **Future Shock:** Economic expansions don't last forever. If you haven't built a solid financial foundation during good times, you'll be more vulnerable to the hardships of an eventual downturn.

3. **Risky Investments:**

    - **The "Get Rich Quick" Mentality:** The "everything goes up" mentality during expansions can tempt you towards risky investments promising high returns. This could involve chasing hot stocks, investing in unproven ventures, or real estate speculation. You heard my story. Please don't make that mistake.

    - **Potential for High Losses:** These high-risk investments can lead to significant losses if the market takes a turn. Remember, higher potential returns are often accompanied by higher risks.

General Tips:

- **Maintain a Long-Term Perspective:** Don't panic and make drastic changes based on short-term economic fluctuations. Remember, the economy moves in cycles, and downturns eventually give way to expansions.

- **Seek Professional Advice:** A financial coach or advisor can help you assess your risk tolerance and create a personalized financial plan that considers the economic cycle.

- **Stay Informed and Stay Flexible:** Continuously educate yourself about the economy and be prepared to adjust your plans as needed.

Reflection

- How do economic conditions impact your financial situation?
  - Consider how factors like inflation, unemployment, and interest rates affect your income, expenses, and overall financial stability.

- What steps can you take to navigate economic challenges effectively?
  - Think about strategies such as diversifying your income sources, maintaining an emergency fund, and staying informed about economic trends to make informed financial decisions.

Key Takeaways

- Economic cycles are like the weather - constantly changing and unpredictable. Understanding them can help you make informed decisions about your finances.

- Boom times don't last forever, and downturns are inevitable. Building a solid financial safety net is crucial to weathering economic challenges.

- Recognizing the signs of economic cycles can help you adjust your financial plans accordingly, such as increasing savings during expansions and reducing debt during contractions.

- During economic downturns, focus on financial stability by prioritizing essential expenses, boosting income, and managing market volatility.

- In times of economic expansion, be cautious of unsustainable spending habits and risky investments. Stay grounded and focus on long-term financial goals.

You can brave the economic storm since you've learned to navigate the ups and downs. But is simply weathering the storm enough? Financial wellness is about more than just surviving - it's about thriving and creating the life you want. What if you could not only weather the storm but use it to propel yourself toward financial security and freedom? Discover the secrets to building a financial fortress in the next chapter, "Cultivating Financial Wellness."

Chapter Eleven

Cultivating Financial Wellness

*"The difference between ordinary
and extraordinary is that little extra."*
—Jimmy Johnson

You know that feeling? You've been hustling all month, putting in the extra hours, and finally, the weekend arrives. You have some money saved up, a chance to treat yourself to a fancy getaway or a luxurious spa day – pure bliss! But instead of picturing yourself rejuvenated and stress-free, you're stuck in bed, a migraine pulsing behind your eyes and a fever making every movement feel like a chore.

This, my friend, is a perfect example of why financial wellness goes beyond just having money in the bank. It's about feeling secure and empowered by your finances because money is a tool for experiencing life, not a cage that traps you in worry.

Think about it – even if you had booked that extravagant trip while feeling stressed about your finances, would you have truly enjoyed it? The nagging doubt (the "what-ifs" about your allocation decisions) would likely linger, dimming the experience.

Before we dive in, **what really is financial wellness?**

Put simply, financial wellness is the ability to manage your money effectively to meet your current needs and future goals. It's financial literacy, financial independence, financial security, and confidence successfully balanced together with you as a priority at the center of it all—taking care of yourself mentally, physically, and emotionally while progressively building a financial portfolio that serves your future best.

The Relationship Between Physical and Mental Health and Financial Wellness

When I think about financial wellness, I think about Sam's story. He was a fantastic salesman, consistently exceeding targets and bringing in major revenue. However, he prioritized work above all else. He rarely took breaks, skipped meals to close deals, and wouldn't take a sick day even when clearly under the weather.

At first, it seemed like his strategy was working. He was a top performer, raking in the bonuses and commissions. But slowly, things started to change. The constant stress and lack of self-care took a toll on his health. He ended up catching a nasty case of pneumonia that required hospitalization. Not only did he miss weeks of work, but the medical bills were a huge financial burden. It took him months to recover both physically and financially.

Sam's story is a lesson. While prioritizing work can bring short-term gains, neglecting your health can lead to significant financial setbacks down the road.

Financial planning isn't just about saving for retirement or a house. It's about creating a secure and fulfilling future. And a key part of that future is your health and well-being. **Here's how they are connected:**

Health impacts your finances:

- **Medical bills:** Unexpected medical costs can derail even the best financial plans. Preventive care and a healthy lifestyle can help reduce the risk of chronic diseases and expensive treatments.

- **Earning potential:** Good health allows you to work, be productive, and potentially earn a higher income. Conversely, health issues can limit your ability to work and impact your earning potential.

Finances impact your health:

- **Stress of financial worries:** Financial stress can lead to unhealthy habits and worsen existing health conditions.

- **Affordability of healthcare:** Without proper financial planning, you might forgo necessary healthcare due to cost concerns.

The good news: If you take care of both your health and finances, **you create a positive feedback loop:**

- **Financial security reduces stress:** Knowing you have a financial safety net can improve your mental and physical well-being.

- **Healthy habits save money:** Investing in preventive care and healthy habits can prevent costly health problems down the road.

Incorporating Health into Financial Planning

Here are some tips for intertwining your health and well-being goals with your financial plan:

1. **Budgeting for health:**

    - **Track your health spending:** Monitor how much you spend on healthy groceries, gym memberships, doctor visits, and vacations. This will help you allocate appropriate funds in your budget.

    - **Prioritize preventive care:** Factor in regular checkups, and screenings. Early detection of health issues can save money on treatment down the line.

    - **Invest in healthy habits:** Budget for healthy food options, fitness classes, or equipment you'll use regularly.

2. **Financial tools for well-being:**

    - **Health savings account (HSA):** If available through your employer, contribute to an HSA. You can save pre-tax dollars for qualified medical expenses, essentially getting a tax break to prioritize your health.

    - **Disability insurance:** Consider disability insurance to protect your income if illness or injury prevents you from working. This ensures your financial security isn't jeopardized by health issues. As mentioned in Chapter 1, I became disabled almost 3 years ago. It took a toll on me physically, mentally, and financially. While I had disability insurance, I still saw how quickly I could go from feeling relatively secure to panicked and anxious over money. Be sure to grab my book "*Limitation to Limitless: 7 Proven Strategies To Surviving Disability Without Going Bankrupt*". It will be an eye-opener on the importance of long-term disability.

3. **Long-term planning for well-being:**
   - **Retirement healthcare costs:** Factor in potential healthcare costs like long-term care or medication needs when planning your retirement savings.
   - **Healthy lifestyle goals:** Consider how your financial plan can support long-term health goals. Maybe you want to save for that dream weight-loss surgery or a yoga retreat.

A healthy you is a financially secure you. These tips will help you create a financial plan that supports your overall well-being for today and the future.

How to Manage Stress and Anxiety Related to Finances

Common Sources of Financial Stress and Anxiety

Financial stress and anxiety are, unfortunately, common experiences. **Here are some of the frequent culprits that can trigger these feelings:**

1. **Debt:** Student loans, credit card debt, mortgages, and other forms of debt can feel overwhelming and create a constant burden.

2. **Job insecurity:** The fear of losing your job or facing income instability can be a major source of anxiety.

3. **Living paycheck to paycheck:** Having little to no financial buffer can cause significant stress, especially when unexpected expenses arise.

4. **Rising costs of living:** The increasing cost of essentials like housing, food, and healthcare can make it difficult to make ends meet and create a sense of insecurity.

5. **Healthcare costs:** The high cost of medical care, even with insurance, can be a significant source of stress and anxiety.

6. **Major life events:** Events like job changes, starting a family, or caring for aging parents can strain your finances and lead to stress.

7. **Lack of a financial plan:** Not having a clear understanding of your income, expenses, and financial goals can make it difficult to feel in control of your finances and lead to anxiety.

8. **Societal pressures:** Keeping up with the Joneses or feeling pressure to maintain a certain lifestyle can create financial strain and anxiety.

These are just some of the common sources of financial stress and anxiety. The specific triggers will vary depending on your circumstances. However, it's important to recognize the signs of financial stress and take steps to manage them before they negatively impact your well-being.

To get personal for a minute. When I became disabled in 2021, my financial safety net gave me a sense of security. I had two long term disability policies, plus an emergency fund covering close to a year of expenses. But then, everything seemed to go wrong. A construction project went way over budget. A tenant turned into a squatter, who as of the writing of this book has not paid rent in over 18 months. Costs incurred for a sick family member were hundreds and sometimes in the thousands monthly. My Uber Eats bills skyrocketed because I couldn't cook. Those were just a few of the curveball that life threw my way.

I was also building my business and felt the need to keep going. I rationalized that if my disability persisted, I could work on my own schedule. I had planned to eventually transition to my business full time at some point in the short to medium term anyway. I was optimistic that in a few months, I'd be better. Life had other plans. Eventually, it all became too much to handle. I realized I was crashing and burning fast.

I decided to stop everything in my business, and focus on healing myself and helping my family member heal. On one hand, it was a tough decision. But on the other hand, it was a no-brainer.

Initially, I thought it would only be for a few months. Almost a year later, I am pacing myself to resume.

Financial wellness has been crucial to me throughout this journey. I've had to make sacrifices and sometimes take on debt. Throughout it all, I've continued to prioritize my well-being, taking vacations, going to retreats, hiring a private physical therapist when needed, or treating myself to a massage. I've been living in financial wellness—it's been essential.

Practical Strategies for Managing Stress, Such as Mindfulness, Meditation, and Exercise

When financial worries start to get the best of you, it's important to have some stress-management strategies in your toolbox. I am not a fitness guru, and I couldn't run anymore after my accident. Still, I know how much meditation and relaxation helped me during my period of disability. You should identify a couple of things to do to help you get your head straight when you begin to waiver in stress.

Here are a few techniques that can help you manage financial stress and anxiety:

Mindfulness and Relaxation Techniques:

- **Mindfulness:** Mindfulness practices help you focus on the present moment and detach you from worries about the future or regrets about the past. This can be particularly helpful when financial anxieties start to spiral. Techniques like mindful breathing exercises or short meditations can help you center yourself and gain perspective. There are many free guided meditations available online and on apps to help you get started.

- **Deep breathing:** Taking slow, deep breaths is a simple yet powerful way to calm your nervous system and reduce stress. When you're feeling overwhelmed, focus on your breath, inhaling for a count of four and exhaling for a count of six. Repeat this for several minutes until you feel calmer.

- **Progressive muscle relaxation:** Tense and relax different muscle groups in your body, one at a time. This can help release the physical tension that often accompanies stress and anxiety.

Exercise and Physical Activity:

- **Regular exercise:** Physical activity is a well-known stress reliever. Engaging in regular exercise, even just a brisk walk for 30 minutes a day, can release endorphins, improve mood, and reduce stress hormones. Find an activity you enjoy, whether it's running, swimming, dancing, or team sports.

- **Yoga:** Yoga combines physical postures, breathing exercises, and meditation. It's a fantastic way to reduce stress, improve flexibility, and promote overall well-being. Many yoga studios offer beginner classes, or you can find online yoga routines to follow at home.

How Reducing Stress Can Improve Financial Decision-Making and Overall Well-Being

Chronic financial stress can cloud your judgment and lead to impulsive decisions that worsen your financial situation. It only takes a couple of bad decisions to undo the hard work that you have put in.

Reducing stress can improve your financial decision-making and overall well-being in the following ways:

Clearer Thinking and Better Choices:

- **Reduced impulsivity:** When stressed, our brains are more likely to seek immediate gratification, leading to poor financial choices like unnecessary spending or taking on high-interest debt. Reducing stress allows for calmer, more rational thinking, enabling you to make sound financial decisions based on long-term goals.

- **Improved focus:** Financial stress can make it difficult to concentrate, hindering your ability to analyze financial information effectively. Lower stress levels improve focus, allowing you to carefully consider your options and make informed financial choices.

Increased Motivation and Positive Action:

- **Empowerment and control:** Financial stress can feel overwhelming, leading to a sense of helplessness. Reducing stress fosters a sense of empowerment and control over your finances. You'll be more motivated to tackle financial challenges, create a budget, and stick to your financial plan.

- **Long-term planning:** Chronic stress makes it difficult to think about the future. When calmer, you can set clear financial goals and develop strategies to achieve them. You'll be more likely to prioritize saving for retirement or long-term needs.

When you feel calmer and more in control, you'll make better financial decisions, which in turn leads to greater financial security and further reduces stress.

Investing in Personal Growth and Development for Long-Term Financial Wellness

When it comes to building financial wellness, we often think about saving money and making smart investments. But there's another crucial investment you can make: investing in yourself. **Here's why prioritizing personal growth and development is key to achieving long-term financial security:**

Boosting Earning Potential:

- **Skill development:** Learning new skills or enhancing existing ones can make you a more valuable asset in the workplace. This can lead to promotions, raises, or opportunities for higher-paying jobs, significantly increasing your earning potential.

- **Career advancement:** Investing in relevant education or certifications can open doors to new career paths with better earning potential.

Making Smarter Financial Decisions:

- **Improved financial literacy:** Learning about personal finance, budgeting, investing, and debt management can empower you to make informed financial decisions. You'll be better equipped to save for your goals, invest wisely, and avoid costly financial mistakes. If you are ready to go deeper into learning about personal finance and building wealth, you can always reach out to me at Tanya@growyourwealth10x.com.

- **Increased confidence:** Personal development fosters self-confidence and a growth mindset. This can help you overcome challenges, negotiate effectively, and advocate for yourself in financial situations, leading to better financial outcomes.

Building a Fulfilling Career Path:

- **Increased job satisfaction:** When you invest in skills and knowledge that align with your interests and passions, you're more likely to find a career you enjoy. This intrinsic motivation can lead to higher productivity and greater earning potential in the long run.

- **Reduced stress and burnout:** Feeling stuck in a dead-end job can be a major source of stress. Investing in yourself opens doors to new possibilities and career paths, reducing job dissatisfaction and burnout, which can negatively impact your overall well-being and financial security.

Examples of Investments in Personal Growth:

- **Education:** Consider pursuing a degree, certificate program, or online courses to develop relevant skills.

- **Professional development workshops or conferences:** Stay updated on industry trends and best practices.

- **Mentorship programs:** Gain valuable guidance and insights from experienced professionals.

- **Books, audiobooks, and online learning resources:** There's a wealth of knowledge available on personal finance, business, and skill development.

Investing in yourself is an ongoing process. If you make the time and resources for personal growth, you are laying the foundations of a secure and financially stable future.

Reflection

- How does your overall well-being impact your financial decisions?
    - Consider how your physical, emotional, and mental health influences your financial choices. For example, stress or anxiety may lead to impulse spending, while a sense of security and well-being can promote mindful financial habits.
- What steps can you take to cultivate greater financial wellness in your life?
    - Think about practical actions you can take to improve your financial wellness, such as creating a budget, setting financial goals, practicing self-care to reduce stress, and seeking professional advice if needed.

Key Takeaways

- Financial wellness goes beyond having money in the bank; it's about feeling secure and empowered by your finances.
- The relationship between physical and mental health and financial wellness is interconnected, impacting both your health and finances.

- Incorporating health into financial planning includes budgeting for health, using financial tools for well-being, and long-term planning for well-being.

- Managing financial stress and anxiety is crucial for making sound financial decisions and overall well-being.

- Investing in personal growth and development boosts earning potential, improves financial literacy, and leads to a fulfilling career path.

- Cultivating greater financial wellness involves considering how your overall well-being impacts your financial decisions and taking practical steps to improve financial wellness.

Wrapping up our journey to financial wellness, the final chapter, "Giving Back and Leaving a Legacy," explores how financial security empowers you to make a positive impact. We'll delve into strategies for charitable giving, explore options for leaving a lasting legacy, and discuss how financial planning can contribute to a life filled with purpose and meaning.

Chapter Twelve

Giving Back and Leaving a Legacy

*"We make a living by what we get,
but we make a life by what we give."*
— **Winston Churchill**

I remember the worn linoleum floor of the children's hospital felt cold and sterile beneath my feet. I wasn't there as a patient but as a volunteer, a nervous woman with a stack of coloring books under my arm. The air hung heavy with a mix of antiseptic cleaner and worried whispers.

Spotting a woman hunched over a plastic chair, her face etched with worry, I approached hesitantly. Her child, a little boy no older than five, lay pale and listless in the bed. The woman's eyes were red-rimmed, her hands twisting in her lap.

Mustering my courage, I offered a small smile and asked if they'd like some coloring books. The woman's face lit up, a flicker of hope replacing the worry. The boy perked up slightly, his eyes widening at the sight of bright pictures.

For the next hour, I sat with them. I wasn't a doctor or a nurse, but I could offer a listening ear and a distraction. The little boy, whose name was Ethan, slowly warmed up, giggling as we colored dinosaurs and spaceships. His mother, relieved momentarily, shared stories about Ethan's love for drawing rockets.

Leaving that day, the weight of the hospital seemed lighter. Ethan's weak smile stayed with me as I waved goodbye. It wasn't a grand gesture, just a small act of kindness in a difficult time. Yet, the feeling of warmth that bloomed in my chest was unlike anything else.

This was close to 3 decades ago, and while that experience was not my first taste of giving back, it was my first time doing so in a hospital. It wasn't about the coloring books but about offering a sliver of comfort in a sea of worry. It taught me the profound impact of even the smallest act on another person and the deep sense of fulfillment that comes from helping others.

Since I was a teenager, volunteering has become an important part of my life. Whether it's working with special needs children, mentoring adults and younger children about financial education, or sitting on nonprofit boards, that feeling of contributing to something bigger than myself never ceases to amaze me. It's a reminder that true happiness lies not just in what we get but in what we give.

The Ripple Effect: Giving Back and Finding Fulfillment

There's a certain magic that happens when we step outside ourselves and contribute to the well-being of our community. It's not just about helping others, although that's certainly a crucial aspect. Giving back fosters a profound sense of personal fulfillment that enriches our lives in unexpected ways.

Imagine this: you're at a local soup kitchen, helping out for the first time. The clatter of dishes mixes with the murmur of conversation as you serve steaming bowls of stew to those in need. A weary-looking man smiles gratefully, his eyes crinkling at the corners. It's a small interaction, but it leaves a mark.

This is the essence of giving back. It's the realization that even a seemingly insignificant act can create a ripple effect. That bowl of stew might be just the sustenance someone needs to get through the day. Your presence and willingness to lend a hand might be a beacon of hope in a difficult time.

However, the benefits extend far beyond the recipient. **Here's how giving back impacts your sense of fulfillment:**

Emotional Rewards:

- **Connection and Purpose:** We are social creatures wired to feel a sense of belonging. Contributing to our community fosters a connection with others and a sense of purpose that transcends individual goals. It reminds us that we're part of something bigger than ourselves.

- **Increased Happiness:** Studies show that helping others triggers the release of endorphins, the body's natural feel-good chemicals. This translates to a boost in mood, reduced stress, and a heightened sense of happiness.

- **Personal Growth:** Stepping outside your comfort zone and volunteering your time or skills can develop new talents, expand your perspective, and build confidence. Giving back can be a catalyst for personal growth.

Psychological Growth:

- **Increased Self-Esteem:** Contributing to the well-being of others validates our worth and fosters a sense of accomplishment. Stepping outside our comfort zone to volunteer or advocate for a cause builds confidence and allows us to see ourselves as capable agents of change.

- **Gratitude and Perspective:** By helping those less fortunate, we develop a deeper sense of gratitude for our blessings. Witnessing the challenges others face can shift our perspective and make us appreciate the good things in our lives even more.

Legacy and Meaning:

- **Leaving a Positive Mark:** Leaving a legacy is about creating a lasting impact that extends beyond your lifetime. Knowing your actions have a ripple effect and contribute to a better future can be incredibly fulfilling. This sense of purpose transcends personal gain and connects us to the greater good.

- **Passing on Values:** Philanthropy and legacy planning are opportunities to instill your values in future generations. Whether it's supporting educational opportunities or environmental causes, we can use our resources to shape the world according to your principles. This ensures your values continue to guide your descendants and have a lasting influence.

Giving back doesn't require grand gestures. It can be as simple as volunteering at a shelter, mentoring a student, or organizing a neighborhood clean-up. Even small acts of kindness can have a profound impact.

The feeling of fulfillment that comes from giving back is a gift – a gift you give to yourself and the community around you. It reminds you that true happiness lies in connection, purpose, and making a positive difference, no matter how small. So why not start creating your ripple effect today?

Making a Difference: Ways to Give Back and Find Your Cause

The desire to give back to your community is a powerful motivator, but translating that desire into action can be daunting. Over the years, **I have found different ways to get involved and find causes that resonate with me; these can help you too:**

Avenues for Giving Back:

- **Volunteering:** This is a classic way to directly contribute your time and skills. Food banks, animal shelters, after-school programs, and senior centers are just a few organizations that often rely on volunteers.

- **Donating:** Financial contributions are essential for many charitable organizations. You can donate to a specific cause you care about or support a local umbrella organization that funds various initiatives.

- **Mentorship:** Sharing your knowledge and experience with someone younger can be incredibly rewarding. Programs exist to mentor students, young professionals, and even at-risk youth.

- **Advocacy:** Raise your voice for a cause you believe in! Contact your local representatives, write letters to the editor, or participate in peaceful protests.

- **Fundraising:** Organize a charity event like a bake sale, car wash, or community walk to raise money for a specific cause.

- **Starting a Foundation:** For those with significant resources, establishing a charitable foundation allows you to create a lasting impact on a cause you're passionate about.

Finding Your Cause:

- **Reflect on Your Values:** What issues are most important to you? Is it environmental protection, animal welfare, education access, or social justice? Identifying your core values will help you narrow down potential causes.

- **Explore Local Needs:** What are your community's pressing issues? Are there local organizations addressing those needs? Researching local charities can be a great starting point.

- **Skills and Interests:** Consider how you can leverage your skills and interests to give back. Do you enjoy working with children? Are you passionate about technology? There are likely organizations that could benefit from your unique talents.

- **Talk to Others:** Ask friends, family, or colleagues about causes they support. Volunteering alongside someone you know can be a great way to get started.

The most important thing is to find a cause that ignites your passion. When you give back in a way that aligns with your values and interests, the experience becomes truly fulfilling.

Establishing a Legacy Plan for Future Generations

Legacy planning goes beyond simply writing a will. It's a comprehensive strategy to ensure your wealth and values not only reach future generations but also have a lasting positive impact. **Here's a breakdown of this important concept:**

What is Legacy Planning?

Think of legacy planning as building a bridge between your life and the lives of your loved ones. **It's about:**

- **Financial Planning:** Distributing your assets (money, property) in a way that aligns with your wishes and minimizes tax burdens for your beneficiaries.

- **Value Transfer:** Passing on your core values, beliefs, and principles to future generations. This can be through family discussions, written documents, or even establishing charitable foundations that reflect your values.

Why is Legacy Planning Important?

- **Secures Financial Future:** A well-crafted legacy plan ensures your loved ones inherit your wealth responsibly and have the necessary resources to thrive.

- **Preserve Values:** Legacy planning allows you to shape the future by ensuring your values continue to guide your descendants.

- **Reduces Family Conflict:** Clear communication about your wishes through a legacy plan can minimize disagreements and ensure a smooth inheritance process.

- **Creates Lasting Impact:** By incorporating charitable giving, you can extend your legacy beyond your family and contribute to causes you believe in.

How Does Legacy Planning Work?

Several tools can be used to build a solid legacy plan:

- **Wills and Trusts:** Legal documents outlining how your assets will be distributed after your death. Trusts can offer additional benefits like asset protection and control over how funds are used.

- **Beneficiary Designations:** Specifying who inherits specific assets like retirement accounts or life insurance policies.

- **Charitable Giving:** Donating funds or assets to causes you care about, either during your lifetime or through your estate.

- **Family Communication:** Openly discussing your values, financial situation, and wishes with your family can foster understanding and prepare them for the future.

Important Note: Legacy planning is an ongoing process. Your plan should be reviewed and updated regularly to reflect changes in your life, family dynamics, and financial situation.

Creating Your Legacy Plan: A Step-by-Step Guide

Here's a roadmap to get you started, **with actionable steps to create a legacy plan and involve your family:**

Step 1: Gather Information:

- **Inventory Your Assets:** List everything you own, including property, bank accounts, investments, and retirement savings.

- **Review Existing Documents:** Gather copies of your will, trusts, insurance policies, and beneficiary designations.

- **Consider Your Goals:** What do you want your legacy to be? How do you want your assets and values to be passed on?

Step 2: Craft the Cornerstones:

- **Last will:** This legal document outlines how your assets will be distributed after your death. Consider consulting an estate planning attorney to ensure it meets your specific needs.

- **Durable Power of Attorney:** This document allows you to designate someone you trust to make financial decisions on your behalf if you become incapacitated.

- **Healthcare Power of Attorney (or Advance Directive):** This document allows you to appoint someone you trust to make medical decisions for you if you are unable to do so yourself.

- **Living Trust**: Trusts can offer benefits like asset protection and control over how funds are used. Depending on your situation, a revocable living trust or a charitable trust might be suitable options. Discuss these with your attorney.

- **Create a Family Mission Statement:** This document captures your core values and guiding principles. It can be a powerful tool for future generations to understand your priorities and use them to make decisions. Involve your family in brainstorming and drafting this statement.

Step 3: Involve Your Family:

- **Schedule a Family Meeting:** Openly discuss your financial situation, your wishes for your legacy, and the estate planning documents you've created.

- **Explain Your Decisions:** Help your family understand the reasoning behind your choices regarding asset distribution and charitable giving.

- **Assign Roles:** Designate an executor for your will, someone responsible for handling the legal aspects after your death. You also want to appoint a healthcare proxy and a guardian for minor children, if applicable.

- **Keep it Updated:** Schedule regular family meetings to review and update your legacy plan as your life circumstances change.

Step 4: Ensure Your Wishes Are Carried Out:

- **Store Documents Securely:** Keep your will, trusts, and other essential documents in a safe deposit box or a secure location accessible to your executor. Provide a copy of the location to your executor.

- **Communicate Clearly:** Reiterate your wishes with your family throughout your life. Open communication minimizes confusion and ensures a smooth transition after your passing.

- **Consider Professional Help:** An estate planning attorney can guide you through the legal complexities and ensure your plan is legally sound.

The Importance of Aligning Your Financial Goals with Your Values and Priorities

Aligning your financial goals with your values and priorities is crucial for creating a fulfilling and successful financial future. It's about moving beyond just accumulating money and towards building a life that reflects what truly matters to you.

Here's why it's important:

Clarity and Direction:

- **Focus on What Matters:** Understanding your values – security, freedom, experiences – can help you set clear financial goals that support those values. This provides a roadmap for your financial decisions, ensuring you're working towards something meaningful.

- **Prioritization:** There will always be competing financial demands. Aligning your goals with your values helps you prioritize where to allocate your resources. It becomes clear whether that new gadget aligns with your value of saving for travel or if it's a distraction.

Motivation and Sustainability:

- **Intrinsic Drive:** Financial goals tied to your values are inherently more motivating. Saving for a dream vacation feels different than saving for "someday". The connection to your values fuels your desire to achieve your financial goals.

- **Long-Term Commitment:** Financial plans built solely on external pressures (keeping up with the Joneses) are more susceptible to derailment. When your goals are rooted in your values, you're more likely to stay committed for the long haul.

Reduced Stress and Increased Satisfaction:

- **Mindful Spending:** Knowing your values helps you avoid unnecessary spending on things that don't truly matter. This reduces feelings of guilt and frees up resources for what you truly value.

- **Financial Peace of Mind:** Aligning your finances with your values creates a sense of control and purpose. You're not just chasing numbers; you're building a future that aligns with your deepest desires.

Here's how to get started:

After identifying your core values through introspection, life experiences, and even online assessments, **your next step is to:**

- **Translate Values into Goals:** Turn your values into actionable financial goals. For example, if "family" is a core value, a goal might be saving for your children's education.
- **Evaluate Spending Habits:** Track your expenses and see if they align with your values. Are you spending on things that truly bring you joy, or are there areas to adjust?
- **Create a Values-Based Budget:** Develop a budget that allocates funds towards your financial goals and activities that reflect your values.

Your values and priorities may change over time. In any case of significant change, revisit your financial plan regularly and adjust it accordingly.

You can live a purposeful, fulfilling, and financially secure life by aligning your finances with your values.

Reflection

Alignment With Values and Principles:

- How do your daily spending habits reflect what you truly value in life?
    - Reflect on your recent purchases and consider whether they align with your core values and long-term priorities.
- Are there any areas where your financial decisions seem to contradict your principles?
    - Identify instances where your spending may not align with your short-term or long-term goals, and explore why this misalignment exists.

Legacy and Future Generations:

- What financial habits and practices do you want to pass down to future generations?

  - Consider the lessons you've learned about money management and how you can instill positive financial behaviors in your family or community.

- In what ways can your current financial decisions shape the opportunities and security of future generations?

  - Imagine the impact your financial choices today could have on the lives of your children, grandchildren, or even society as a whole, and reflect on the legacy you hope to leave behind.

Key Takeaways

- **Alignment with Values and Principles:**

  - **Reflect on Your Spending:** Regularly assess your spending habits to ensure they align with your core values and long-term priorities.

  - **Identify Misalignments:** Recognize areas where your financial decisions may contradict your principles and explore ways to address these discrepancies.

- **Legacy and Future Generations:**

  - **Pass Down Positive Habits:** Consider the financial habits and practices you want to pass down to future generations, focusing on instilling positive behaviors.

- **Shape Future Opportunities:** Reflect on how your current financial decisions can impact the opportunities and security of future generations, aiming to leave a meaningful legacy.

There are many ways to seek happiness and fulfillment in life. Financial security is indeed important, but real wealth comes from the relationships we build, the values we uphold, and the good things we do for others. You can leave a lasting legacy by embracing the power of giving back, including philanthropy in your financial plan, and ensuring that your financial goals align with your deepest values.

This book's strategies can unlock your financial potential, propelling you from being broke to building wealth beyond your wildest dreams. But remember, true wealth isn't just measured in dollars and cents. It's the connections we forge, the lives we touch, and the positive impact we leave on the world. So, go forth, armed with knowledge and empowered by your values. Start building your legacy today - one that extends far beyond the bottom line.

Moving Forward Together

The Ripple Effect of Financial Literacy

*"We make a living by what we get,
but we make a life by what we give."*
— Winston Churchill

So, we've been on quite a journey together, haven't we? We discussed setting clear goals, tackling debt, and building a strong financial foundation. We learned how to shift our mindset for success and embraced the importance of budgeting and saving. We even built an emergency fund (hopefully!) and explored ways to increase our income.

But remember, this isn't a one-shot deal. Financial literacy is a lifelong adventure. As your life changes, so will your financial needs. The key is to keep learning, staying informed, and adapting your strategies as you go.

The good news: The knowledge you've gained here empowers you to take charge of your financial future. You can make informed decisions, build a secure life, and even achieve that dream of financial freedom. Don't stop here! Keep exploring and keep learning!

Beyond the Numbers

Imagine money as a toolbox. Financial literacy teaches you what tools are in that box and how to use them effectively. Sure, a big toolbox with fancy gadgets might be impressive, but if you don't know how to use any of them, it's not very helpful. Financial literacy empowers you to go beyond just collecting financial tools (money) and shows you how to use them to build the life you truly want. This could be anything from feeling secure knowing you have an emergency fund, to finally taking that dream vacation you've been saving for, or even giving back to causes you care about. It's about using your financial knowledge to build a life that aligns with your values and goals.

Financial Literacy is a Journey

Financial literacy isn't a one-time class you take and forget. It is like learning to ride a bike. Once you get the hang of it, you can pretty much cruise along. But just like with riding a bike, things can change. Maybe you move to a hillier area or decide to take on some epic mountain trails. That means you might need to learn some new skills or get a different bike altogether.

As your life progresses, your financial situation will change too. Maybe you get married, have kids, or start a business. These changes might require you to learn new financial concepts or adjust your strategies.

There's always more to learn! There are tons of resources available online, in libraries, and even through workshops to keep you up to speed.

You wouldn't try to climb Mount Everest on a tiny tricycle, right? Sometimes, on your financial journey, you might need expert help. Financial coaches are like experienced cyclists who can show you the best routes, help you avoid potholes, and even give you a little push when you need it.

Taking Action: Turning Knowledge into Progress

From Book Smarts to Real-World Results

Financial literacy is powerful, but it's only the first step. The magic happens when you put what you've learned into action! Think of this book as your financial roadmap—now it's time to grab the steering wheel and hit the road.

Small Steps, Big Results

Don't get overwhelmed by the big picture. Setting clear financial goals is great, but achieving them is all about taking smaller, actionable steps. Maybe it's setting up an automated transfer to your savings account or finally tackling that pile of receipts to identify spending leaks. These small steps add up over time and keep you moving forward.

Celebrate Your Victories

Building financial security is a marathon, not a sprint. There will be bumps along the road, but take a moment to celebrate your milestones, big or small. Reaching a savings goal, paying off a debt, or simply sticking to your budget for a month - all these achievements deserve a pat on the back. Recognizing your progress keeps you motivated and reminds you how far you've come.

Final Thoughts and Inspiration

The true wealth you build isn't just measured in dollars and cents. Financial success is about creating a fulfilling life that aligns with your values and dreams. This book has equipped you with the knowledge and tools to achieve that.

Confidence and a Positive Mindset

Taking control of your finances can feel overwhelming at times. But remember, you've already taken a big step by learning the basics. Approach your financial journey with confidence, knowing you have the power to make positive changes. A positive mindset will fuel your motivation and help you overcome challenges along the way.

A Call to Action

Just another reminder if you have not yet started because you think you don't have enough.

Remember at the beginning of the book, I told you I came to America with $100, at sixteen, alone and undocumented. I started budgeting with the $75 that I made weekly and I had to pay $20 weekly rent from it. Yet, I purchased my first home at 25. I built my retirement to 7 figures before 48. There were countless obstacles and setbacks that I faced every step along the way, even today with my disability. My point is, if I waited until I thought I was ready, it would have taken a very long time to start. If I got discouraged and gave up, I wouldn't be where I am today.

Don't wait for the "perfect" time to start. Take action today! Start by completing all the exercises in the workbook. Next, join my community at growyourwealth10x.com **to take** your knowledge even deeper. This is your chance to build a legacy that extends far beyond your bank account. Embark on your wealth-building journey with excitement, and watch your dreams become reality!

Let's Do This!